GLENRAVEL LOCAL HISTORY PROJECT
ASHTON CENTRE
5 CHURCHILL STREET
BELFAST
BT 15 2BP

The Glenravel Local History Project is an independent and self supporting local history group based in North Belfast. It is a non-political and non-religious group with its interests being in nothing more but our local and factual history. We are not grant maintained by any government body either British or Irish and our entire aim is to bring an understanding and an awareness of Belfast's local history to those who we feel it belongs - the ordinary people of this city.

"The histories of mankind that we possess are histories only of the higher classes."

T. R. Malthus
The Principle of Population, II, 1798.

GW00566288

Glenravel Local History Project
1994

FOREWORD

BY
JOE BAKER
GLENRAVEL LOCAL HISTORY PROJECT

Today there is a new and determined interest in the subject of local history. This new interest is generated by those within society to whom it was thought local history did not belong - the working class. For decades we were told that this subject was to be studied by those who belonged to the so called upper classes, but recent years have brought about the working class element who are now beginning to compile the histories of their individual close knit communities and A District Called The Bone is one of them. This book is unique due to the fact that it was sponsored by local businesses within that area and not by any government department through grant assistance. Many government bodies have been set up to promote books such as this but, as has been the case many times before, they only promote written histories which are suitable to them and their select few.

A District Called the Bone is a fascinating account of this area's history and it is one which has been tirelessly researched by Michael Liggett. It informs us how the area received its name, or to keep on the safe side, what the different versions are and continues by giving a detailed history. Included are accounts of the various problems which affected the area from the Belfast troubles of 1920-1922 through to the German Luftwaffe blitz of 1941 in which many parts of the area were destroyed. We are informed of the area's industry in which the people worked and of other "industries" which survived because of the locals and which included the famous pawnshops and 'chippies.' Pubs and Clubs also receive a mention, as do the numerous sporting activities which the people of the area took part in and no Belfast area's history would be complete without its ghost story. At the end of the book Michael has compiled a short list on the growth of the Bone which begins with the establishment of a bleaching green in 1790 and ends with the redevelopment of the area in 1980. There is no doubt that the people of the Bone will find this a brilliant read and we are hoping that the neighbouring people in Ardoyne will not be waiting long before they enjoy a similar read.

INTRODUCTION

When I first moved to Havana Street in 1971, the present phase of the troubles was at its height and although this was a very dangerous area, it wasn't long before I realised that there was another conflict taking place. To every wee fella from around these streets this conflict was just every bit as important; the difference between being from The Bone or Ardoyne. Havana Street was on the border of these two areas. The side with the odd numbers was in The Bone, while the side with the even numbers was in Ardoyne. Being from the Bone meant I lived in Sacred Heart Parish and so I went over "The Brickyard" to St. Columban's School. "The Bone Hills" were our playground and Havana Street's gang guarded it's territory to the best of their ability against the many street gangs from Ardoyne. As I grew older I have listened to many heated debates about The Bone and Ardoyne so I decided to put as much information to- gether as possible about both areas. The first of these publications is about The Marrowbone and I hope it will make many people realise just how much of the old Bone has virtually gone. Landmarks like "The Fieldy Wall", Lindsay's Mill, McAleenan's Yard, Ferguson's Shop, to name just a few are now only memories. The new Bone is now completely redeveloped with newly laid out streets with many new families. I hope this publication will help people realise how rich and important our history is.

Special thanks have to go to Joe Baker, Co-ordinator of the Glenravel Local History Project, for all his help. The General Board and staff of the New Lodge Ashton Centre for their continuing help and support. The staff of the Linenhall Library and Belfast Central Library. The production of this book would not have been possible without the help and encouragement of the many older residents of the Bone who are too numerous to mention here.

Michael Liggett 1994

A DISTRICT CALLED THE BONE

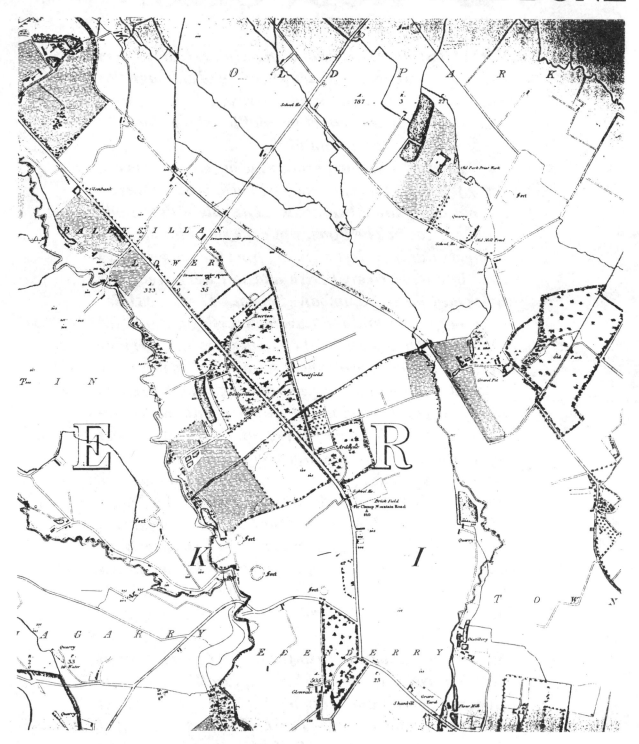

NORTH BELFAST 1830

Where are you from ? Everyone has heard of.....the man from God knows where? However, have any of us stopped to think about it? He must have come from somewhere; some town, some townland, or some parish. Everywhere in Ireland has a name. Placenames let us know a lot about the character of those who live there, even though some of those characteristics may be misplaced. If you are from The Bone then you are certainly different from everyone else in this city. Many's the argument that has taken place when someone has carelessly referred to a person from The Bone as an Ardoyne man or woman. People from The Bone are proud of where they are from and will point out distinctly, who they are!

This publication will attempt to show how The Bone grew up as a self-contained little 'village' so to speak; an independent district; unique and distinctly different from every other area in this city.

The area has been called The Bone or The Marrowbone since it's inception in the 1860's even though officially the government authorities have consistently referred to the area as Oldpark. To understand how it came to be called The Bone / Marrowbone we have to look at the subject from two aspects; a Gaelic one and an English one.

A lot of local names originate from the Gaelic description of the area. Years ago, all government in Ireland was conducted by English-speaking people. The majority of people who lived here spoke in Gaelic. They did not read or write in English because they did not need to. Subsequently placenames in Ireland were written in English the way they are pronounced in Gaelic. We therefore have ended up with names which only the ardent Gaelic scholar can decipher and translate. Names such as:
Derry.........was originally Doire..........which means The Oak Grove
Belfast.....was originally Beal Feirsde, or The mouth of the sandy ford.
Shankill...was originally Sean Chill, or The old church.
Ardoyne...was originally Ard Eoin, or The heights of Owen (or John).

Other places were named after the people who funded them and others got their names from nick-names.

There are three possible suggestions as to the origin of the name Marrowbone/Bone. No one knows for sure which one is correct but I shall present all three arguments and you can judge for yourself.

Firstly, the name could have come from the Gaelic origin. Many placenames in Ireland have the word Maghera prefixing them. This could easily be spelt as Marrow. In Belfast this would have been pronounced as Marra. Marrowbone could just as easily have been a corruption of Machaire Boin. This translates as 'the plain of the cow'. Other place names with the word Maghera (Machaire) prefixing them are; Magherafelt, Maghreamourne, Magheralin, Magheraveely.

Secondly, 'Marrowbone could have come from a mere nickname. Local folklore insists that there was once a rag and bone yard in Ardilea Street. Subsequently those who worked there were called 'the Bone Men',or 'the Marrowbone men'. This was later used to refer to people from the Bone or Marrowbone.

Thirdly, there is a story that once there was a settlement of French Monks in this area and they erected a shrine to Our Lady in the locality. She was known as Marie Le Bon. It is said that Marrowbone is a corruption of this name. Unfortunately there is no evidence surviving of this shrine today.

As I said earlier, no-one knows for sure how the area got it's name. You can decide for yourself.

The Marrowbone or The Bone as it is now called, is a small area in North Belfast, situated on the slopes of Squire's Hill

and Cavehill at Oldpark. The area is steeped in history and it is remarkable how it has survived until now. I intend to tell the history of this small district as precisely as possible before it is forgotten forever.

The wooded slopes leading up to the peak of Cavehill is where the majority of people lived long before Belfast was established. The Cavehill was crowned by a fortification called Mac Art's Fort, which was a central point for the inhabitants of those days. The correct Gaelic name for Cave Hill is Ben Madaghan (Madigan's Point). The hill stands at a height of 1,142 ft. above sea level and overlooks most of Belfast. It is reputed to be the place where The Inauguration Throne of the O'Neill clan stood. The stone on which this ceremony took place was known as 'The Giant's Chair'. The story of this chair had been common folk history in the area which was once the kingdom of the O'Neill Clan.

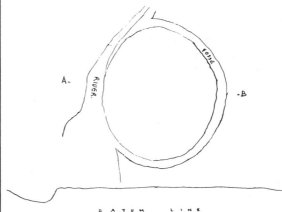

REPORT ON THE FORT AT OLDPARK BY FRANCIS JOSEPH BIGGER

Many earth forts existed on the lands now contained in the city of Belfast, and in no district were they so common as about Oldpark, Edendaire and Ard-Eoghan. There is one, still in a fine state of preservation, close to a newly laid out street on the Oldpark Road, immediately west of the yard of the old Lyon's house. It will soon be built over. Such a small site should be preserved and treasured as a small open space by the Corporation of Belfast. As its fate is so certain we give a plan and section of it as it exists at present. Its fosse (moat) could have been easily filled with water from an adjoining stream now put into factory uses.

Seen in outline against the sky, from any part of the city, it presents the appearance of a recumbent human profile....This crag descends on the side next to Belfast Lough in a sheer precipice; on the other side it is entrenched, and was used as a fortress by ancient Irish clans. On the very verge of the precipice some large stones were piled together so as to form a seat.
In December 1896 the chair was destroyed by vandals who toppled the structure over the cliff. No fewer than fifteen

raths or ringforts run in a line from Glencairn, Ligoneil, Ardoyne, and Oldpark up to Mac Art's Fort on the Cave Hill. This was once the stronghold of the O'Neills, one of the great Irish clans. The surname is still popular today. In fact many of the Belfast placenames still retain their Gaelic title; Ligoneil (O'Neill's hollow), Castlereagh {O'Neill's grey castle), Ballymacarrett (the town of the son of Art O'Neill), Clandeboy (the clan of fair-haired Hugh O'Neill), Connswater (named after Conn O'Neill). Mac Art's Fort was one of the last strongholds of Brian Mac Art O'Neill, who with his clan were exterminated by Chichester in the name of the English Crown. He then proceeded to confiscate the lands on which Belfast now stands as the spoils of war. In fact it has been claimed that ' not a rood of the land on which Belfast is built, or all of Ulster , for that matter, is in the possession of it's rightful owners.'

Evidence that the Oldpark area in particular had been occupied at that time has all but been destroyed. There were two ringforts in the area. The first was situated behind what was known as Oldpark House, the residence of W. J. Lyons, a wealthy landowner. The site was allowed to be built over many years ago. Today there is a school and youth club at the ancient site at Oldpark Terrace, Deanby.

The second rath or ringfort was situated at the Deerpark Road. It would have been located where the river runs behind the houses to feed the now vacant Egg Factory. Is it a coincidence that both forts were on the same river? It is unfortunate that this second fort has also been destroyed by developers. It is incredible that such ancient fortifications should be allowed to be destroyed seeing as they form such an important part of our heritage. The only proof we have of these historical sites today are their placements on old ordinance survey maps.

The ascension of Elizabeth to the throne of England heralded the subjugation of Ireland. The O'Neills were finally defeated and it was not until after this happened that a settlement was established on the marshy ground around the end of the Farset River. This was an ideal spot as it was close to the end of a natural deep water harbour. Belfast started here. The first street to appear was High Street, which remains today, even though it has changed dramatically through the years. The Farset at one stage flowed openly down the middle of the street and ships came up as far as where Bridge Street is today. Belfast is a corruption of the words Beal Feirsde (the mouth of the sandy ford). By 1613 expansion had begun in earnest. The city was 'owned' by the Chichester Family, who gave themselves the grand title of Marquis of Donegal.

In 1611 it is recorded that the Chichester family fenced off a large area of land at Oldpark. Here they had a large house built which became known as The Lodge. This large enclosure was stocked with fallow deer and was the first known deerpark in The North. As Belfast grew, a highway led north out of the city to this hunting lodge. The road became known as The Lodge Road. Another lodge was built in the vicinity however and The Lodge Road became known as The Old Lodge Road. The upper stretch of this road became known as The Oldpark Road.

The original Lodge was situated beside the ringfort at what is now Oldpark Terrace. It was later to become known as Oldpark House, the residence of the wealthy Lyons Family from around 1750. These large hunting grounds are still recalled today by Deerpark Road and Oldpark Road.

The earliest form of census for the area was taken in 1659. North Belfast's results were as follows;
Townlands of Edenderry, Ballysilly and Laganeile:- 66 people. {43 English and 23 Irish}
Townlands of Balleghan, The Oldpark and part of Listillyard:- 24 people {13 English and 11 Irish}
Townlands of Cloghcastle, Newparks and Skeggan Earl:- 38 people { 20 English and 18 Irish}

Belfast continued to grow. Linen mills started to spring up around the city. One of the first industries to open at Oldpark was the Bleach Greens of Robert Howie. The abundance of streams and rivers in the locality made it an ideal location for the development of factories and mills. The Chichester Family by this stage had sold most of their lands to wealthy businessmen to raise monies to clear their debts. Some of these businessmen saw that the acquisition of lands at Oldpark would be an investment and so industrialists came to these areas. One such businessman opened a paper-staining factory where The Jamaica Inn now stands.

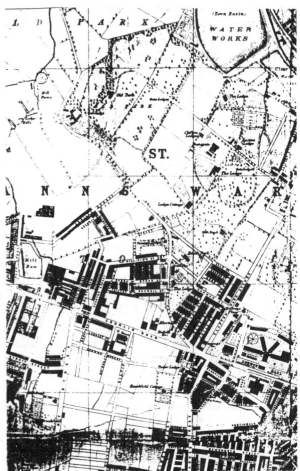

MAP OF 1880 SHOWING NORTH BELFAST

Names.		Description of Tenement.	Area.		
Townlands, Streets, & Occupiers.	Immediate Lessors.		A.	R.	P.
TOWNPARKS— continued.					
OLD-PARK-ROAD—con.					
OLD-PARK-TERRACE.					
(Ord. S. 4.)					
Henry Joy M'Cracken,	William Ware,	Ho., yd., & sm. garden,		—	
Henry Hodginson,	Same,	Ho., yd., & sm. garden,		—	
Captain Hand,	Same,	Ho., yd., & sm. garden,		—	
William Ware,	Immediate Lessor,	House, offices, & garden,	0	2	14
(Vernant-lodge.)					
(Ord. S. b.)					
James M'Tier,	Marquis of Donegal,	House, offices, and land,	11	1	22
John Tate,	Gen. John Ashmore, Col. Chas. Ashmore, Lewis Ashmore,	Land,	5	0	22
William Lees,	James Sherlock,	Land,	5	0	38
(Valued with No. 11 New-lodge-road.)					
John Tate,	William T. B. Lyons,	Land,	10	0	23
William Ewart,	Edward Jones Smith,	Land,	14	0	0
James Johnston,	William Ewart,	House,		—	
Susan Bailey,	Same,	House,		—	
(Valued in Townland of Old-park.)					
CRUMLIN-STREET.					
(Ord. S. 14.)					
(Valued in Townland of Edenderry.)					
(Valued in Townland of Edenderry.)					
Christopher M'Farren,	William S. Mitchell,	House and yard,		—	
Philip Smith,	Same,	House and yard,		—	
EVERTON-STREET.					
(Ord. S. 14.)					
(Valued with No. 83 Crumlin-road.)					
John M'Cready,	James Bradford,	Land,	1	2	20
William Ware,	Same,	Land,	1	2	35
.	Same,	House (in progress) and yard,		—	
.	Same,	House (in progress) and yard,		—	
.	Same,	House (in progress) and yard,		—	
.	Same,	House (in progress) and yard,		—	
.	Same,	House (in progress) and yard,		—	
.	Same,	House (in progress) and yard,		—	
.	Same,	House (in progress) and yard,		—	
.	Same,	House (in progress) and yard,		—	
.	Same,	House (in progress) and yard,		—	
William Ewart,	Reps. Blackiston Houston,	Building-ground (waste),	0	1	6
William Ewart,	Trustees of Thos. Scott,	Land,	0	2	22
EWART'S-ROW.					
(Ord. S. 14.)					
John Hanley,	William Ewart,	House and yard,		—	
Eccles Gordon and another,	Same,	House and yard,		—	
James Woodcock,	Same,	House and yard,		—	
Margaret Spence and another,	Same,	House and yard,		—	
John Galt,	Same,	House and yard,		—	
OLD-PARK-ROAD.					
(Ord. S. 14, 21, & 22.)					
William Dobbin,	Marquis of Donegal,	Land,	8	2	30
(Old-lodge-house.)					
(Ord. S. 14 & 15.)					
John Lytle,	Robt. Patterson Elliott and John M'Dowell Elliott,	House, offices, and land,	12	2	0
(Park-lodge.)					
(Ord. S. 14.)					
Hugh Andrews,	James Bradford,	House, offices, and land,	2	1	38
(Beech-park.)					
(Ord. S. 14.)					
John Getty,	In fee,	House, offices, and land,	4	0	28
John Getty,	George Dunbar,	House and land,	6	0	24
(Lodge-cottage.)					
(Ord. S. 14.)					
James Coleman,	John Hind,	House, offices, & garden,	1	0	0
James Hind,	Thomas Scott,	Gate-lodge and land,	5	2	14
(Valued in Townland of Old-park.)					
(Old-park-cottage.)					
(Ord. S. 14.)					
Michl. John Andrews,	William Ware,	House, offices, & garden,	2	0	15
William Ware,	Thomas Scott,	Office and garden,	0	0	30
Passage to 45 and 47 Everton-street.					
OLD PARK.					
NEW-LODGE-ROAD.					
(Ord. S. 7.)					
(Valued in Townland of Townparks.)					
William T. B. Lyons,	In fee,	Ho., offs., yard, & land,	29	0	33
(Valued in Townland of Townparks.)					
OLD-PARK-ROAD.					
(Ord. S. 1, 7 & 14.)					
(Valued in Townland of Townparks.)					
George Thompson,	Jane Anderson,	Ho., offs., yard, & land,	39	2	12
John Lough,	Rev. Octavius Glover,	Ho., offs., yard, & land,	15	0	25
John Beatty,	Same,	Land,	13	0	22
Thomas Verner,	Cave-hill Railway Co.,	21 lineal perches of Cave-hill Railway,		—	
John Magee,	William Hicks and Robert Walker,	Land,	7	1	38
(Valued with No. 13 New-lodge-road.)					
John Magee,	Robert Walker,	Land,	11	0	18
LOW-LODGE-MILLS.					
(Ord. S. 7.)					
Unoccupied,	William Hicks and Robert Walker,	Old print works & yard,		—	
Grant and Thompson,	Same,	Corn-mill,		—	
OLD-PARK-ROAD—con.					
Thomas Kirk,	William Hicks and Robert Walker,	House,		—	
Henry Irwin,	Same,	House,		—	
Grant and Thompson,	Same,	House,		—	
Henry Gallagher,	Same,	House,		—	
John Fulton,	Same,	House,		—	
Felix Gormil,	Same,	House,		—	
(Valued with No. 13 New-lodge road.)					
(Valued with No. 17 Old-park-road.)					
		Waste under houses, roads, & sm. gardens,	7	1	27

GRIFFITH'S VALUATION OF TENEMENTS 1860

The province of Ulster contained nine counties. Within these counties large numbers of Protestant farmers held their land under more favourable conditions than the native Irish Catholics. When the potato blight hit Ireland and the 'famine' was enforced on the poor, Ulster lost 16% of it's population. These losses fell exclusively on the native Irish Catholics. In despair the survivors fled the land and headed for America, England, Scotland and Belfast. The majority of these people were poor tenant farmers. Belfast at the time was becoming an important industrial port. This wealth and prosperity, however, was not evenly distributed amongst the inhabitants.

The history of Belfast prior to 1850 had been marred by hunger riots. The Poor House at Clifton Street was well established and the graveyards had already got large plots of paupers graves and cholera pits. When the migration of poor tenant farmers took place, those in search of a better life, 'jumped from the frying pan into the fire', so to speak. If they got a job, and that was highly unlikely, they only earned enough to survive, while they had to live in the most squalid living conditions imaginable. Rural Catholics had been coming into Belfast in a steady stream and districts such as Carrick Hill, The Pound and The Docks became grossly overcrowded. The emergence in Belfast of the Presbyterian cleric, Rev. Dr. Henry Cooke encouraged sectarianism. When the Repeal of the Union Movement began, led by Daniel O'Connell, Cooke vigorously opposed it. His anti-Catholic, anti-Nationalist speeches led to serious riots in Belfast which subsequently resulted in death and injury. Belfast people began to divide themselves into two factions, Nationalists and Unionists. The majority of Nationalists were Catholics and the majority of Unionists were Protestants. The end of the 1850's saw the first major outbreak of sectarian rioting in Belfast. Working class areas in Belfast have been segregated along these lines right down to the present day. One observer of the situation compared the scene to two starving dogs fighting for scraps from the master's table, as abject poverty in Belfast was the same in all working-class areas.

1860 witnessed the first real valuation of land and property in Ireland. It became known as Griffith's Valuation of Tenements. Every field and building in the whole of Ireland was listed and valued. The Oldpark was mentioned but The Bone/Marrowbone as we know it, was not even there. Ewart's Row and Everton Street had just been built. Ewart's Mill was there. The big houses on The Oldpark Road are listed but the area was principally fields listed as the Townparks.
The main land-owners are listed;

The Marquis of Donegal - 19 acres, 3 roods and 58 perches.
Wm. T. B. Lyons - 39 acres, 23 roods and 33 perches.
Jane Anderson - 39 acres, 2 roods and 12 perches.
Wm. Hicks and Robert Walker - 18 acres, 1 rood and 56 perches.

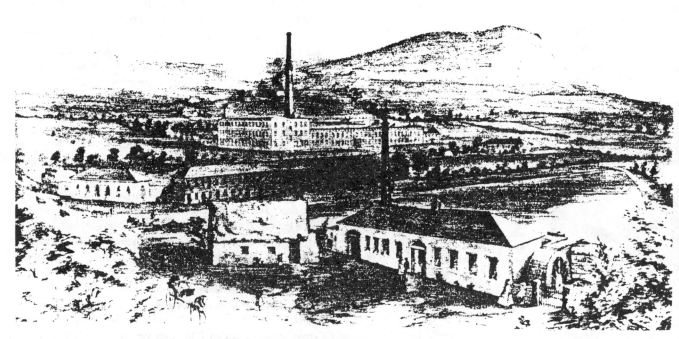

OLDPARK MILL

IN 1800 IT WAS LYON'S LINEN BLEACH MILL BUT BECAME Mc PHERSON'S COTTON PRINTWORKS IN 1824. IN THE FOREGROUND ARE COTTAGES BUILT FOR EMPLOYEES, LATER KNOWN AS OLDPARK TERRACE, AND A FLAX BEETLING MILL POWERED BY WATER FROM THE MILL DAM BEHIND. A SCHOOLHOUSE HAS BEEN BUILT TO THE LEFT OF THE COTTAGES.

COURTYARD OF THE MANSION HOUSE AT OLDPARK AROUND 1935

Rev.Octavius Glover - 15 acres.
Edward Jones Smith - 14 acres.
Robert Patterson Elliot and
John McDowell Elliot - 12 acres and 2 roods.
James Sherlock - 5 acres and 38 perches.
General John Ashmore and
Colonel Charles Ashmore - .5 acres and 22 perch

Starting at Vernant Lodge which was situated where the road turns between Louisa Street and Hillview Street (where Anderson's Blinds is now located), there were 11 acres of land belonging to The Marquis of Donegal. It contained a house, offices and land. Next came the property of the Ashmore's, 5 acres in all. This was next to 5 acres belonging to James Sherlock. It was here that the area we now call The Bone, started. According to Griffith's Valuation the Printworks Factory was unoccupied at this stage. This was located where The Jamaica Inn now stands. A cornmill was in operation beside the factory.

The first street in The Bone was built for the mill-workers of Savage's Flax-Spinning Mill. This mill later became known as Prospect Mill. Savage's Row had 39 houses and it was in these houses that the first people in the Bone lived. The year was 1868.

By 1870 another 9 houses were built on the other side of the row. By this stage most of the Lower Oldpark Road had not been developed. In fact, from Savage's Row to Carr's Glen there was only the odd cottage scattered here and there. Listed in the street directory at the time was a grocery store on the Lower Oldpark Road owned by J. Boyd. This store also doubled up as the district Post Office. Oldpark Printworks are also listed. This business was run by W.Girdwood & Co. The area still retains the name today with Girdwood British Army Camp.

By 1880 Savages Row had changed yet again with the arrival of Wallace's Brick and Tile Manufacturers. The row had been re-named Ardilea Street. Ardilea was the name of the Jordanstown residence of Sir John Savage, the local flax-mill owner. There were 80 houses in the street by 1880, including Armstrong's Spirit Grocery Store. Another four streets had been built; Antigua Street (it had 20 houses, including Brown's Pub), Rothsay Street (it had 5 houses.), Saunderson's Street and Glenpark Street (both of which contained a number of small houses.)
There were also two wells listed in the area. One behind Ardilea Street beside the Brick Factory. The other, a larger well, was situated at the corner of Ardilea Street and Glenpark Street. The residents from The Bone drew water from both wells for many years.

In 1890 Finiston School opened on the Oldpark Road. The previous year Sacred Heart Roman Catholic Church opened on the corner of Oldpark Road and Glenview Street. Building within the little streets of the Bone was continuing constantly and by the end of 1890 every street was complete. Another industry opened next to Wallace's

Brickworks. The Irish Match Company was established in 1895.

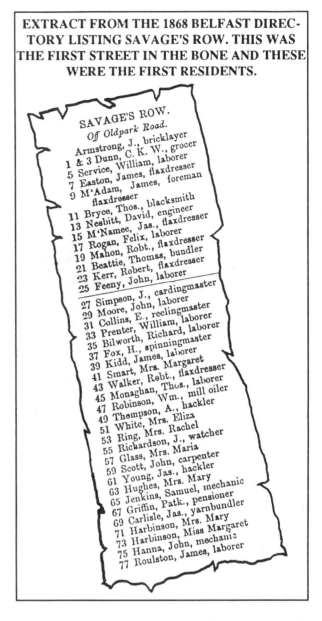

EXTRACT FROM THE 1868 BELFAST DIRECTORY LISTING SAVAGE'S ROW. THIS WAS THE FIRST STREET IN THE BONE AND THESE WERE THE FIRST RESIDENTS.

SAVAGE'S ROW.
Off Oldpark Road.
Armstrong, J., bricklayer
1 & 3 Dunn, C. K. W., grocer
5 Service, William, laborer
7 Easton, James, flaxdresser
9 M'Adam, James, foreman flaxdresser
11 Bryce, Thos., blacksmith
13 Nesbitt, David, engineer
15 M'Namee, Jas., flaxdresser
17 Rogan, Felix, laborer
19 Mahon, Robt., flaxdresser
21 Beattie, Thomas, bundler
23 Kerr, Robert, flaxdresser
25 Feeny, John, laborer
27 Simpson, J., cardingmaster
29 Moore, John, laborer
31 Collins, E., reelingmaster
33 Prenter, William, laborer
35 Bilworth, Richard, laborer
37 Fox, H., spinningmaster
39 Kidd, James, laborer
41 Smart, Mrs. Margaret
43 Walker, Robt., flaxdresser
45 Monaghan, Thos., laborer
47 Robinson, Wm., mill oiler
49 Thompson, A., hackler
51 White, Mrs. Eliza
53 Ring, Mrs. Rachel
55 Richardson, J., watcher
57 Glass, Mrs. Maria
59 Scott, John, carpenter
61 Young, Jas., hackler
63 Hughes, Mrs. Mary
65 Jenkins, Samuel, mechanic
67 Griffin, Patk., pensioner
69 Carlisle, Jas., yarnbundler
71 Harbinson, Mrs. Mary
73 Harbinson, Miss Margaret
75 Hanna, John, mechanic
77 Roulston, James, laborer

By 1899 there was a well established farmyard where the R.U.C. Barracks is now situated at Torrens Avenue. The area then was just fields stretching up into the hills with another couple of factories up at Deanby. A Beetling Mill operated where Cliftonville Circus is now situated. In fact, Westland Road was once called Beetling Mill Lane. Further up the Oldpark Road roughly at where the Model School is now located , was The Oldpark Printworks. It was in 1899 that Finiston Post Office was first listed on the Oldpark Road. It was located roughly where Rooney's Butchers is now. Havana Street, Kingston Street and Ardoyne Avenue were built in 1900. At the same time, St.Sila's Church was opened beside the Farmyard. These were only temporary premises as a new and more permanent church was being built at the corner of Oldpark Road and Ardoyne Avenue. The new St.Sila's Church opened in 1902, the same year as Holy Cross Roman Catholic Church opened at Ardoyne. A lecture hall was built with St.Sila's Church. The site is now occupied by a

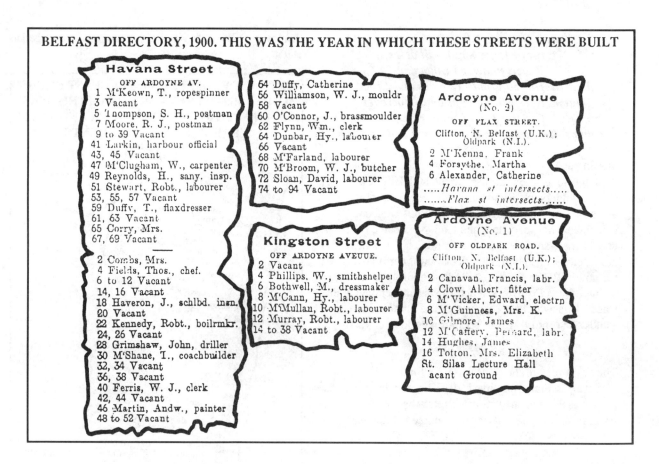

BELFAST DIRECTORY, 1900. THIS WAS THE YEAR IN WHICH THESE STREETS WERE BUILT

Havana Street

OFF ARDOYNE AV.

1 M'Keown, T., ropespinner
3 Vacant
5 Thompson, S. H., postman
7 Moore, R. J., postman
9 to 39 Vacant
41 Larkin, harbour official
43, 45 Vacant
47 M'Clugham, W., carpenter
49 Reynolds, H., sany. insp.
51 Stewart, Robt., labourer
53, 55, 57 Vacant
59 Duffy, T., flaxdresser
61, 63 Vacant
65 Corry, Mrs.
67, 69 Vacant

2 Combs, Mrs.
4 Fields, Thos., chef.
6 to 12 Vacant
14, 16 Vacant
18 Haveron, J., schlbd. insn.
20 Vacant
22 Kennedy, Robt., boilrmkr.
24, 26 Vacant
28 Grimshaw, John, driller
30 M'Shane, T., coachbuilder
32, 34 Vacant
36, 38 Vacant
40 Ferris, W. J., clerk
42, 44 Vacant
46 Martin, Andw., painter
48 to 52 Vacant

64 Duffy, Catherine
56 Williamson, W. J., mouldr
58 Vacant
60 O'Connor, J., brassmoulder
62 Flynn, Wm., clerk
64 Dunbar, Hy., labourer
66 Vacant
68 M'Farland, labourer
70 M'Broom, W. J., butcher
72 Sloan, David, labourer
74 to 94 Vacant

Kingston Street

OFF ARDOYNE AVENUE.

2 Vacant
4 Phillips, W., smithshelper
6 Bothwell, M., dressmaker
8 M'Cann, Hy., labourer
10 M'Mullan, Robt., labourer
12 Murray, Robt., labourer
14 to 38 Vacant

Ardoyne Avenue
(No. 2)

OFF FLAX STREET.

Clifton, N. Belfast (U.K.);
Oldpark (N.I.).

2 M'Kenna, Frank
4 Forsythe, Martha
6 Alexander, Catherine
.....Havana st intersects.....
.......Flax st intersects.......

Ardoyne Avenue
(No. 1)

OFF OLDPARK ROAD.

Clifton, N. Belfast (U.K.);
Oldpark (N.I.).

2 Canavan, Francis, labr.
4 Clow, Albert, fitter
6 M'Vicker, Edward, electrn
8 M'Guinness, Mrs. K.
10 Gilmore, James
12 M'Caffery, Bernard, labr.
14 Hughes, James
16 Totton, Mrs. Elizabeth
St. Silas Lecture Hall
Vacant Ground

---

public house, Francie's. In 1906 Belfast Free Public Library was opened at the corner of Century Street and Oldpark Road. The building is still used as a library today. With the building of the Glenview Street Schools in 1921 and then the Parochial Hall in 1924, The Bone was more or less complete.

One street was never completed even though it had a nameplate on the wall where it was supposed to be. That street was called Manilla Street.

What were known locally as the Bally Streets, were constructed in 1895.

Ballyclare Street	Ballymena Street
Ballynure Street	Ballymoney Street
Ballycastle Street	Ballycarry Street

These streets housed Protestant families exclusively until the advent of the present phase of the troubles. After severe rioting in the area sectarian boundaries were redrawn. Heathfield /Torrens was built in the 1930s. Torrens Avenue was the final street to be built in 1935. At about the same time Ardilea Drive , a row of just five houses, was built in the Bone. The Park Cinema was built in 1936. The next major industry to come to the Bone was The Mourne Clothing Factory. This factory was built at Ardoyne Avenue in 1952. The playing pitches on the Oldpark Road were developed in 1966. Finally in 1967 St. Gemma's Secondary School for girls was opened on the brickyard between the Bone and Ardoyne.

Today the complete area has been redeveloped. The only buildings which remain from those days are the Parochial Hall, Sacred Heart Church and the Presbetry in Glenview Street.

By 1885 the numbers of Catholics residing in the Oldpark area was multiplying rapidly, especially around the narrow streets of the Bone. The demand for church services in the area became so great that the residents organised the Mass to be held in a disused building in Antigua Street, which was originally used as a pub. A priest from St. Patrick's, Fr. Crickard, began to celebrate Mass here regularly. The building was eventually used as a school-house. A better school was built nearby and Mass was said on these premises while the church was built. When the structure was completed it was distinctly different from most other churches as it had a round tower incorporated in the building. The Church of The Sacred Heart was dedicated by Bishop Mc Allister in 1889. A Parochial House was built beside the church in Glenview Street. The first priest to reside there was Fr. Bernard Faloona and he took charge of the church as administrator. The district was raised to the status of a parish in 1905 and the first Parish Priest was Rev. H. O'Boyle. The district continued to grow steadily and when Fr. O'Boyle died in 1906 Canon O'Neill was appointed to take his place.

The need for better education facilities was never greater. A permanent school was required as soon as possible. However, due to a dispute between the Board of National Education and the Catholic Church authorities, work could not start until 1920. The situation at the temporary school had by this time become a disgrace. In the girl's school for instance, only one large room was available. In this room 200 children were divided into five standards. To compound the problem the walls were crumbling, there were many broken windows and the building was in such a dilapidated state that the Medical Officer for the Health Board eventually intervened in the dispute. By this time unfortunately the First World War had begun and all building works had been suspended. When the green light was given in 1920 the building took less than a year to complete.

While the new schools were being built at Glenpark Street pupils were taught in a hut in Gracehill Street where the Parochial Hall now stands. The schools were completed in 1921 at the height of the troubles. Girls and boys from the area could now be educated in comparative comfort. The classrooms were well lighted and were heated throughout with hot water pipes and radiators. A spacious playground and a roof garden meant that classes could be held outside in the summer months.

The Parish Priest who oversaw much of this work was Fr. James K. O'Neill from Ballycastle, Co. Antrim. He came to Sacred Heart Parish from St. Patrick's in 1906. He was a founder member of The Knights of Columbanus and of An Colaiste Comhghaill, and though not a fluent Gaelic speaker himself, Canon O'Neill was a pioneer and ardent supporter of the Irish Language Movement. He died in Sacred Heart Presbetry on Sunday, March 19th 1922, probably as a result of the anxieties and horrors associated with the Pogroms. His position was filled by a Glensman called Fr. J. Mc Auley. He unfortunately inherited a parish which had been devastated by a prolonged campaign of sectarian violence. He appealed for help from the Bishop at the time

" the Catholics of Sacred Heart Parish are hemmed in on all sides by a hostile population. They were practically in a state of siege for between two and three years. As a result of this prolonged bombardment 244 families, comprising over 1,000 souls, were compelled to abandon their homes, in many instances losing all their belongings, but glad to escape with their lives; 57 houses were burnt to the ground; and 17 Catholics lost their lives. In addition to those who were driven out by violence many families who could afford to do so removed to other parts of the city, and some families left the city altogether." Fr. J. Mc Auley. P.P.
Indeed, by 1922 the situation was so tense that the Bishop of Down and Connor, the Rev. Dr. Mac Rory visited the area to see the destruction for himself. Luckily an organisation existed at that time called The Belfast White Cross Society. This organisation relieved the situation by building a street of new houses. At that time it was common practice in Belfast for families to live in what were known as half houses. That is, one family lived upstairs and another lived downstairs under the one roof. The houses in the Bone were constructed of red brick with slate roofs. Running cold water was eventually supplied by The Corporation as was a town gas supply. Most houses had two small bedrooms, a living room and a scullery. The toilet was in an out-house in the yard. It was these cramped conditions which prompted the residents to approach the new Parish Priest to build a Parochial Hall, 'not merely as a place of recreation but also as a refuge from the intoler-

able congestion of their homes.'

It was a difficult and costly task as most of the wealthier families had fled from the parish. The task was a necessity however and on completion the hall could be used to help raise money to pay the debts incurred from building the church and schools. The money was eventually raised by three principle sources; Rev. Dr. Mac Rory, The White Cross Society, and the contributions from the people of the Bone. The Parochial Hall was completed in 1924 and still stands today, an impressive structure, it is as central to life in the parish today as it was then.

PHOTOGRAPHS TAKEN AT THE LYON'S MANSION AT OLDPARK AROUND 1930

"ON AN AUGUST NIGHT BY THE MOONS BRIGHT LIGHT IN A DISTRICT CALLED THE BONE"

THE POGROMS

In the Home Rule years the National Volunteers were organised throughout Ireland. A company of the National Volunteers was organised in the Bone in 1913. The captain was Owen Mc Kernan, a teacher at Glenview Street School. They drilled regularly in the school grounds under the instruction of Mr. J. Mc Nally . With the advent of World War One the National Volunteers split. The majority left to fight for the British Army in Belgium or France. The remainder formed the Irish Volunteers, who eventu

ally fought at the Easter Rebellion in 1916. After the First World War the War of Independence raged in Ireland. A general election resulted in Sinn Fein winning the majority of seats throughout the thirty two counties. In Belfast however, serious sectarian riots brought terror daily to areas like the Bone. Anti-Catholic persecution was at it's height. The events leading up to, and directly following the partition of Ireland has left scars which have turned into the bleeding wounds of today. The Bone was an isolated area hemmed in on all sides by a hostile Unionist population and was practically in a state of siege for the duration of the

SCARED HEART CHAPEL AROUND 1900

1920 Pogroms. Sectarian riots in Belfast seemed to erupt every twelve years from 1850 to 1912. This time however, saw the worst violence in Belfast from it's foundation. The beginning of July 1920 witnessed severe rioting in Derry. The resulting death toll stood at 20 with countless more injured. On July 5th the newspapers were reporting the Connaught Rangers' mutiny. More violence seemed imminent in Derry and subsequently the Twelfth Celebrations in that city were banned. The Orange Order were incensed. Rioting spread quickly to Belfast and on July 21st all the Catholics were chased from their jobs at the shipyards. Three people were killed on the first day of trouble. The following day a Bone-man, Henry Hennessy from Ardilea Street, was shot dead by the military. By the weekend, the death toll in Belfast was eighteen. 500 extra troops from the Duke of Wellington Regiment arrived in the North. On July 28th, The News Letter published a statement barring all republicans from the shipyards.

August was a tense month. The Republican hunger striker, Terence Mc Swiney, was critically ill. The fierce rioting which started at Ballymacarrett quickly spread to the Marrowbone. What happened next heralded a turning point in the troubles. All through July and August Catholics were being evicted from their homes, many escaping luckily with their lives.

In Ewart's Row several people had been intimidated from their homes and all their furniture was stacked in the street and burned. There had been intermittent rioting in the area for several weeks, each riot developing in intensity. According to newspaper reports at the time, the disorder on the 29th August started around midnight and quickly developed into a pitched battle. Revolvers were produced by both sides and a gunbattle developed which lasted into the night. The result of the night's violence was six men dead and over fifty wounded. A Curfew Order was enforced the following day and more British soldiers were drafted into the area. The district was sealed off with barbed wire and the military guarded all the approaches into the area with Lewis guns.

The Daily Mail published the following statement on September 1st....."Now that 20 people have been killed and 400 families burned out of their homes and £1,000,000 worth of damage done, Belfast is beginning to come to it's senses. Belfast is in it's present plight and is faced with future trouble simply and solely because there has been an organised attempt to deprive Catholic families of their homes."

Every day brought more tragedy. On September 10th, Charles O'Neill died from wounds he received on August 29th. Murder Squads had began a reign of terror in the city, killing people in Catholic areas as part of a concerted campaign to intimidate Nationalists and Republicans from their homes. Catholics attacked trams as they ferried workers to the Shipyard. On September 28th and 29th two Protestant shipyard workers were shot dead as they went to work. They were Frederick Blair, (a drill instructer in the U.V.F.) from Louisa Street, and John Lawther, from Everton Street: and so it continued daily throughout Belfast.

In June 1921, Alexander Mc Bride, a member of Sinn Fein from Cardigan Drive, William Kerr from Old Lodge Road and Malachy Halfpenny from Herbert Street were murdered. All three men were taken from their homes during the night by the R. I. C. and their mutilated bodies were discovered the next morning. Terror spread quickly through the parish at the news of this latest atrocity. Sporadic incidents took place around the Bone until December when Michael Crudden was murdered as he came out of Mass at Sacred Heart Church. The year ended with the deaths of David Morrison and Special Constable Francis Hill.

The new year saw regular attacks and counter-attacks in the area. March brought the death of the McMahon's. The following month, loyalists attacked the Bone and destroyed Antigua Street, Rothsay Street and Saunderson's Street. The death toll in the parish stood at seventeen. By the end of June 1922 the total death toll for Belfast was 268 with 244 houses destroyed.

THE BATTLE OF THE MARROWBONE

In July Catholics and even trade unionists were expelled from their work at the shipyards by Unionist Party supporters. Tension was high following the outbreak of rioting in Derry. The parades in that city were banned to prevent further violence. The rioting quickly spread to Belfast. Throughout July and August many determined and vicious attacks were made on the Bone. The inhabitants of the area, according to The Irish News had..."both day and night, right up to the Curfew hours, been terrorised by organised mobs, augmented from distant Orange quarters, attempting to invade the locality wielding revolvers, stones and bottles." The threat of future invasions were made all the more real when people from the area received written warnings to quit their homes. A prominent resident received one such letter stating that...."an attack would be made on the Catholics that week, and the entire place,

MAP OF NORTH BELFAST. 1890

commenced firing into Antigua Street. This heavy machine gun was effective in clearing the street as the rioters and onlookers both dived for cover. At the Mater Hospital several people were admitted; some dead; some seriously wounded; and others not so critically injured.

Neighbours in the Bone say the district was attacked by a mob from Louisa Street at about half one in the morning. A bugle was sounded as a warning and once alerted, all the able bodied men from the area rushed out to defend their homes. The first to die that night was 19 year old Leo Murray from 11 Glenpark Street. He was standing on the corner of Gracehill Street and Glenview Street looking towards Lebanon and Louisa Streets. One shot was fired by a sniper in Ewart's Row and Leo Murray was hit. He fell unconscious in the street amid great panic. Fr. O'Neill, the parish priest, appeared on the scene and gave the last rites. Murray was carried into Mrs. Brown's house until he was brought to the Mater Hospital. He was dead on arrival.

At the Recorders Court, Head Constable Clarke told how after ordering his men to shoot over the heads of the nationalists, he then ordered his men to "shoot into the rioters and aim low so as to get them in the legs." At the same time the military arrived and fired at the rioters. They also fired down Glenview Street from the Oldpark Road with rifles. The rioting continued until about three o'clock in the morning. At 6.30 a.m. Republicans fired from the side of Gallagher's house in Glenpark Street at the police and intermittent firing continued for most of the morning. Two houses in Antigua Street had been burned and most of the houses in the vicinity were damaged.

including the church and other property would be burned." All this intimidation and threats finally erupted into a mini-war on August 29th 1920 which left 6 people dead and over 50 injured. A Recorders Court in Belfast reported fully on that week's riots and especially on the deaths of the men, Murray, Toner, Moan, Kinney, Cassidy and the girl Orr. Mr. Cecil Forde appearing for the military and police described the battle as..."the most serious fighting that had taken place in the history of Belfast." The fighting began between one o'clock and two o'clock on the morning of August 29th. Street lights were put out and shouting and crashing of stones brought police from Leopold Street Barracks to the scene. Head Constable P. Clarke arrived with eight constables and made their way to Antigua Street. Large crowds had been rioting at the Glenpark Street, Glenview Street, Antigua Street junctions. The police immediately charged with batons drawn at the Nationalists from whom someone commenced firing at them with a revolver. The police immediately retreated and sent for their carbines and military help from Victoria Barracks. By this stage the crowds of rioters had dramatically increased with intermittent sniping from both sides. Fearing an imminent invasion of the Bone, someone began to alert the neighbourhood of the impending danger by sounding a bugle. This had the immediate affect of bringing everyone out to defend their homes. The military arrived in an armoured car with a Hotchkiss gun and

A police constable, Richard Evans, from Leopold Street Barracks, stated that he witnessed a crowd rushing down Saundersons Street and Antigua Street into the Unionist quarters where they smashed windows at the top of Ewart's Row. The crowd he estimated at around thirty or forty immediately returned through Antigua Street to Glenpark Street extinguishing all the street lamps as they went. He went on to state that when 'Unionists' came out the rioters began to shoot at them with revolvers. Another constable from Leopold Street Barracks, John Reilly, stated that at about 1.00 a.m. two rival crowds had been rioting at Ewart's Row and Antigua Street. He went on to say that rioting then erupted at the junction of Glenpark Street and Louisa Street. While all this was happening he was caught up between both skirmishes. He began to make his way along Antigua Street to Glenpark Street when someone began shooting at him from the Bone. Almost immediately, the gunfire became more intense and appeared to be directed at the mob who were advancing from Louisa Street, and also at the police at Antigua Street, where two houses were now ablaze. Lieutenant Desmond Martin Fitzgerald, 1st Battalion, Norfolk Regiment, stated that he had been in charge of an armoured car at Antigua Street, Glenpark Street junction. He came under fire almost immediately the military arrived and he commanded his men to open fire with a Hotchkiss gun into Glenpark Street.

Thomas Toner was brought to the Mater Hospital dead. He had been shot through the jaw and neck.

Owen Moans was shot through the heart.

Henry Kinney, died from haemorrhage after being shot in the lung.

W. J. Cassidy was shot twice in the chest. Death was due to perforation of the liver and haemorrhage into the abdominal cavity.

Grace Orr was admitted to hospital the following day, Sunday 30th August. She was suffering from a gunshot wound to the abdomen, but she died eight hours later after doctors battled to save her life.

The people of the area stayed awake all night and gathered on corners the next morning to survey the damage. The threat of further attacks was so great that the Sacred Heart Church remained closed that Sunday. The military remained in position with Lewis Guns on the Oldpark Road facing the church and loyalist residents from the 'Bally Streets' vied with each other to give the soldiers tea and cigarettes. There were many outbreaks of fire during Saturday and Sunday. The targets were mainly Catholic owned spirit-grocery stores. The offices of the Independent Labour Party , facing Ewart's Mill was burned.

Another victim of the night's violence died later from gunshot wounds, Charles O'Neill from Glenpark Street.

OCTOBER 18 1920

August 29th. Even though Police and Military had been on guard to deter further fighting it appears that they were taken completely by surprise by that days events. To begin with, two men, who were helping to remove the belongings of an evicted family at Walton Street were attacked by a gang of youths. The men were accompanied by Constable Mulhern from Leopold Street Barracks. One of the men was stabbed in the head and Constable Mulhern was also hit on the head with a stone. The scene quickly developed into a full scale battle and it wasn't long before the shooting started. The police arrived and began shooting at the rioters and calm was eventually restored with the arrival of an armoured personnel car from Victoria Barracks. During the fight a four year old boy was shot in the shoulder outside his home in Louisa Street. At about five o'clock the rioting was renewed. After a football match at St. Mary's Pitch, Oldpark Avenue, (known locally as the Billiard Table) the supporters made their way home. Passing the Marrowbone a sectarian slagging match began and someone opened fire on the spectators with rifles and revolvers. The military immediately rushed to the scene whereupon the republicans engaged them in a gunbattle. Two men were mortally wounded and a third man, Michael Mc Master from Conlig Street, died when he was knocked down by a military wagon. The other two men were John Gibson of Byron Street and William Mitchell of Downing Street. Eventually the shooting stopped and the police and the military were kept on stand-by all through the night. Several homes in the Bone were raided and seven men were arrested.

April 1922 almost witnessed the complete destruction of the Bone. Loyalists had escalated their campaign against Catholics with bomb attacks throughout the city. From April 14th the Curfew Regulations required that people remained indoors from 11.00 p.m. to 6.00 a.m. Shooting was a common occurrence every day. On Monday 18th a football match had just finished at ' The Billiard Table', (a pitch which was located where the present Sacred Heart Primary School is now situated). It is alleged in newspaper reports at the time that a crowd of spectators returning from the match at about 2.15 p.m. began shooting at Catholics in the Bone. As a result of this shooting a woman called Cissie Wilson was shot in the eye outside her home at 258 Oldpark Road, beside Finiston School. Revolver fire was returned from the streets of the Bone and a riot soon began between the two rival crowds. Police in Lancia cars immediately rushed to the area. Tension remained high throughout the day. On up the road at Cliftonville Circus two B Specials were shot by the I.R.A. at around 3.00 p.m. Sporadic shooting incidents occurred in and around the Bone as a Lancia car continued to patrol the district. One shooting incident resulted with Annie McAuley of Glenpark Street being shot and seriously injured by gunmen shooting from Louisa Street. Raiding parties of police and military spent the greater part of the day searching the area for guns and ammunition. Later that night James Fearon, a 56 year old labourer from Glenpark Street, was shot and seriously injured. William Lavery from Louisa Street, was shot in the hand. By eight o'clock serious rioting had erupted at Ewart's Row. The rioting became so intense that a mob surged forward into the Bone. Antigua Street along with some houses in Rothsay Street and Saunderson Street were set ablaze. The mobs were repelled and the Fire Brigade were summoned to the scene. They fought the blazes for over an hour before they could get the fires under control. They had only left the area an hour when they were summoned again. This time the other side of Antigua Street had been set ablaze. The fire had caught hold and the street was well ablaze by the time the Fire Brigade arrived. They had to spend most of the night quelling the flames amid revolver and rifle fire.

By the morning the area resembled a battleground with the burnt out remains of Antigua Street and parts of Rothsay and Saunderson Streets still smouldering amidst the intermittent sniper fire. Early that morning several people were shot. John Hyland, aged 14, was shot in the face at Ballycarry Street. Daniel Lenaghan of Rosebank Street was shot in the arm. James Cassidy of Park Street was shot in the eye and seriously injured and a boy named Andrew Martin from Ballyclare Street was shot in the wrist. Sniping in the area developed in intensity. James Fearon who was shot the previous night died during the night. A boy named James Smith was shot outside his home at Mayfair Street. A 27 year old man named William Johnston from Louisa Street was shot dead apparently mistaken for a Catholic from the Bone. By the afternoon the area came under intense sniper fire from both the 'Bally streets' and

Ewart's Row. I.R.A. snipers shot three British soldiers at Ewart's Row, one of whom was the Captain commanding the Norfolk Regiment in the district. Loyalist mobs, for the second day running, managed to get into Saundersons Street, where they proceeded to set more houses ablaze. They were eventually repelled. An uneasy calm remained within the district throughout the rest of the week and the military remained posted in the area. Those who were burned out of their houses, thirty families in all, were temporarily accommodated at the green hut behind Brookfield Street. (This was the original Toby's Hall and was situated where the Holy Cross Boys School new canteen is now.) Indeed the situation was that bad that the Bishop for Down and Connor, Rev. Dr. Mac Rory visited the area to see the destruction for himself and to give comfort to his parishioners. Michael Collins in a letter to Sir J. Craig on the 30th of April pointed out that since the 'Pact' (1st April) Catholics killed, 24; Catholic houses burned or looted, 75; Catholic families homeless, 89; Persons homeless, 400; Houses bombed 5. Protestants killed or injured 34; Protestant houses looted or burned, 11. Two Protestants were killed when they were mistaken as Catholics. The Protestant premises were destroyed by loyalists during an outbreak at Marrowbone . The people of the Bone were horrified at the destruction of their district and many fled to live in safer areas.

MAY 1922

On 1st May Annie McAuley who had been shot on April 18th died in hospital. Tension in the area was still high and the military were still in position behind barbed wire and Lewis guns. The district had been effectively sealed off. By May 11th however, the I.R.A. had reorganised in the area and they engaged the Crown Forces in one of the most serious gunbattles ever to have taken place in Belfast. The I.R.A. fired on the British Army from several different positions in gunbattles which lasted for several hours. One newspaper report stated "Military and Police replied to the fire and the rattle of machine guns, the cracks of rifles and the explosions of grenades could be heard all over the city." The following day was Thursday. There had been a brief cessation in the shooting. A bomb exploded however at the Tram Depot at Ardoyne seriously injuring several people. At about 4.00 p.m. a riot started at Antigua Street. As the crowds again attempted to invade the Bone, shooting started. Both sides were exchanging shots at each other and by 6.00 p.m. a fierce gunbattle was in progress. There was only one casualty fortunately, a girl named Mary Ann Mahoney, aged 10, from 3 Gracehill Street. The Bone did receive tragic news that day. A boy called James Smith who had been shot outside his home at Mayfair Street on April 18th died that morning in hospital.

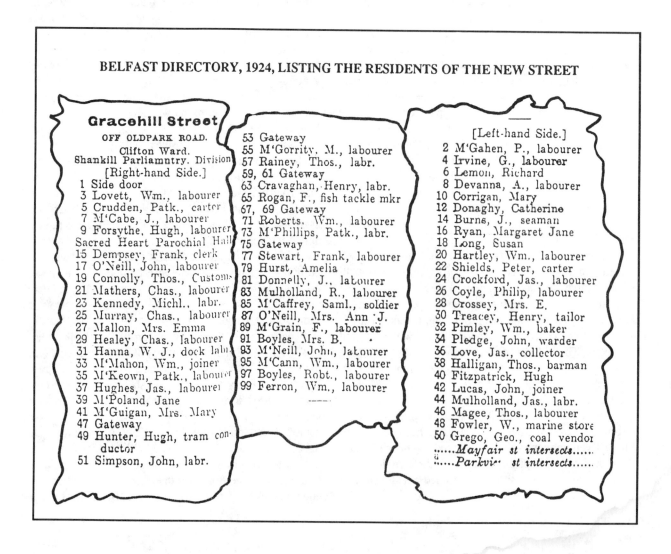

BELFAST DIRECTORY, 1924, LISTING THE RESIDENTS OF THE NEW STREET

Gracehill Street

OFF OLDPARK ROAD.

Clifton Ward.
Shankill Parliamntry. Division

[Right-hand Side.]

1 Side door
3 Lovett, Wm., labourer
5 Crudden, Patk., carter
7 M'Cabe, J., labourer
9 Forsythe, Hugh, labourer
Sacred Heart Parochial Hall
15 Dempsey, Frank, clerk
17 O'Neill, John, labourer
19 Connolly, Thos., Customs
21 Mathers, Chas., labourer
23 Kennedy, Michl., labr.
25 Murray, Chas., labourer
27 Mallon, Mrs. Emma
29 Healey, Chas., labourer
31 Hanna, W. J., dock labr.
33 M'Mahon, Wm., joiner
35 M'Keown, Patk., labourer
37 Hughes, Jas., labourer
39 M'Poland, Jane
41 M'Guigan, Mrs. Mary
47 Gateway
49 Hunter, Hugh, tram conductor
51 Simpson, John, labr.

53 Gateway
55 M'Gorrity, M., labourer
57 Rainey, Thos., labr.
59, 61 Gateway
63 Cravaghan, Henry, labr.
65 Rogan, F., fish tackle mkr
67, 69 Gateway
71 Roberts, Wm., labourer
73 M'Phillips, Patk., labr.
75 Gateway
77 Stewart, Frank, labourer
79 Hurst, Amelia
81 Donnelly, J., labourer
83 Mulholland, R., labourer
85 M'Caffrey, Saml., soldier
87 O'Neill, Mrs. Ann J.
89 M'Grain, F., labourer
91 Boyles, Mrs. B.
93 M'Neill, John, labourer
95 M'Cann, Wm., labourer
97 Boyles, Robt., labourer
99 Ferron, Wm., labourer

[Left-hand Side.]

2 M'Gahen, P., labourer
4 Irvine, G., labourer
6 Lemon, Richard
8 Devanna, A., labourer
10 Corrigan, Mary
12 Donaghy, Catherine
14 Burns, J., seaman
16 Ryan, Margaret Jane
18 Long, Susan
20 Hartley, Wm., labourer
22 Shields, Peter, carter
24 Crockford, Jas., labourer
26 Coyle, Philip, labourer
28 Crossey, Mrs. E.
30 Treacey, Henry, tailor
32 Pimley, Wm., baker
34 Pledge, John, warder
36 Love, Jas., collector
38 Halligan, Thos., barman
40 Fitzpatrick, Hugh
42 Lucas, John, joiner
44 Mulholland, Jas., labr.
46 Magee, Thos., labourer
48 Fowler, W., marine store
50 Grego, Geo., coal vendor
......*Mayfair st intersects*......
......*Parkvi st intersects*......

MEMBERS OF THE WHITE CROSS ASSOCIATON INSPECTING THE 'NEW HOUSES'. 1924

GROUP OF CHILDREN STANDING IN THE 'NEW STREET'. 1924

The following day the I.R.A. opened fire on trams in the Bone. The tram service had to be withdrawn and shooting became so intense that anyone who ventured out did so at their own peril.

A man named Michael Cullen was shot in the chest while walking along Havana Street and died. A conductor who was injured the previous day at the Tram Depot died from his wounds. He was John Mansfield from Groomsport Street.

The shooting recommenced the following day at around 5.00 a.m. when the British Army again came under sustained sniper fire. That morning at 8.00 a.m., William Carmichael from Brookfield Street was seriously wounded when he was shot by the military on the 'Brickyard'. New Curfew Regulations came into operation for the Bone and Ardoyne. All residents within a named boundary were commanded to remain indoors between 9.00 p.m. and 7 a.m. Later that week the I.R.A. brought out the Thompson sub-machinegun for the first time in the troubles at Havana Street.

The Belfast White Cross Association built more houses at Gracehill Street to help house the homeless who were burned out of Antigua, Saunderson, Rothsay and Glenpark Streets. The street was known locally as the New Street and when the Association helped to complete the Parochial Hall, Gracehill Street was finally finished. The year was 1924.

The following is the list of those who lost their lives during the disturbances who lived in the Bone and Oldpark area.

July 22nd 1920; Henry Hennesy, Ardilea St. (R.C.)
Aug. 29th 1920; Henry Kinney, Ardilea St. (R.C.)
Aug. 29th 1920; John Murray, Glenview St.(R.C.)
Aug. 29th 1920; Thomas Toner, Ardilea St. (R.C.)
Aug. 29th 1920; Owen Moan, Glenview St. (R.C.)
Aug. 29th 1920; William Cassidy, Glenpark St. (R.C.)
Aug. 30th 1920; Adam McClean, Southwell St. (Protestant)
Aug. 30th 1920; Grace Orr, Edenderry St. (Protestant)
Sept. 1st 1920; James Couser, Benwell St. (Protestant)
Sept. 10th 1920; Charles O'Neill, Glenpark St. (R.C.)
Sept. 28th 1920; Frederick Blair, Louisa St. (Protestant)
Sept. 29th 1920; John Lawther, Everton St. (Protestant)
Oct. 16th 1920; John Gibson, Byron Place (Protestant)
June 21st 1921; Alexander McBride, Cardigan Drive. (R.C.)
Aug. 31st 1920; John Lee, Manor St. (Protestant)
Sept. 18th 1921; James Johnston, Louisa St.(Protestant)
Dec. 14th 1921; Michael Crudden, Oldpark Rd.(R.C.)
Dec. 27th 1921; David Morrison.(Shot dead on the Oldpark Rd. by the 'Specials')
Dec. 27th 1921; Con. Francis Hill R.I.C. (Shot dead by I.R.A. in the Marrowbone.)
Mar. 24th 1922; William Campbell, Oldpark Avenue. (Protestant)
Mar. 29th 1922; Samuel Mullen, Havana St. (R.C.)
Apr. 14th 1922; William Johnston, Louisa St. (Protestant)
Apr. 14th 1922; James Fearon, Glenpark St. (R.C.)
Apr. 21st 1922; Thomas Best, Louisa St. (Protestant)
Apr. 24th 1922; Ellen Greer, Enniskillen St. (Protestant)
May 1st 1922; Annie McAuley, Glenpark Street (R.C.)

May 12th 1922; Michael Cullen, Havana St. (R.C.)
May 12th 1922; James Smith, Mayfair St. (R.C.)
May 19th 1922; Thomas Boyd, Louisa St. (Protestant)
May 26th 1922; William Toal, Mayfair St. (R.C.)
June 20th 1922; Isabella Foster, Ballycarry St. (Protestant aged 4 months)

A terrible tragedy hit the Marrowbone and surrounding streets when sectarianism was at it's height in the early twenties. As the above list shows, the dead were on both sides. The agony and suffering was shared by everyone. The list unfortunately is only a fraction of those who died in the greater Belfast area. Many more were injured both physically and mentally as Ireland was partitioned. By the end of 1922 the violence gradually abated. The new state called Northern Ireland was established. Emigration became widespread and many men from the Bone left to seek work in England. This trait continues to the present day with many of the district's building workers travelling back and forth from England to the building sites of London. However in the twenties there was work all over England in places such as Coventry, Birmingham, Liverpool etc.

The end of the twenties saw the Stock Market Crash which led to the Great Depression. Rioting broke out on the streets as the poor people of Belfast put their sectarian differences behind them to march together for food and work for all. This harmony of the working class was quickly undermined though by the wealthy employers. Curfew was again imposed and many workers and strikers were shot in what came to be called the Out Door Relief Riots of the Hungry Thirties.

Sectarianism raised it's ugly head again with statements from the then Prime Minister Lord Brookeborough giving the following advice to employers; "There are a great many Protestant and Orangemen who employ R.C.s. I feel I can speak freely on this subject as I have not an R.C. about my own place...I recommend those people who are loyalists not to employ R.C.s, 99% of whom are disloyal."

With statements like this it was quite obvious to those who had survived the 1920 Pogroms that their future was still under threat. The resilience of the people of the Bone was admirable to say the least. They continued to labour away and build up their community throughout all the hard times. However the Thirties were only coming to a close whenever the Second World War broke out.

A DISTRICT CALLED ARDOYNE

THE MOST COMPREHENSIVE HISTORY OF THE ARDOYNE AREA TO DATE

PUBLISHED BY THE GLENRAVEL LOCAL HISTORY PROJECT

AVAILABLE SOON

THIRTY FIVE YEARS OF THE MOVIES

The Park Cinema towers over the Bone. It's shell is now used by a car dealer and a wallpaper and paint shop. In bygone days however it was the centre of entertainment for most of the people from the Bone. It is situated on the Oldpark Road opposite the football pitches and when it was built it had a seating capacity of 1200. This was the largest cinema in North Belfast at that time. The Savoy for instance held 1088 and Crumlin Road Picture House only held one thousand people.

The Park Cinema was built in 1936 two years after The Savoy. (The Savoy was at the corner of Tennent Street and Crumlin Road.) The Forum which now houses The Crumlin Star Social Club was built in 1937, a year after The Park. The cinema business was booming in the thirties and forties and by the time the Bone got it's own cinema there were at least another forty cinemas already in existence in Belfast alone. Some of the bigger ones were:

Broadway (Falls Road)	1380 seating capacity.
The Classic (Castle Lane)	1730 seating capacity.
The Curzon (Ormeau Road)	1500 seating capacity.
The Regal (Lisburn Road)	1270 seating capacity.
The Royal Hippodrome (later known as The New Vic)	1800 seating capacity.
Troxy (Shore Road, later known as The Grove)	1300 seating capacity.
Windsor (Donegal Road)	1250 seating capacity.

Sadly everything must come to pass and with the development of television and video, the cinema eventually went out of fashion. By 1970 the Park Cinema's seating capacity was down to 642 and it eventually closed it's doors in 1972, the last cinema to do so in North Belfast.

THE PARK CINEMA OPENED ITS DOORS AT CHRISTMAS 1936. HERE IS ONE OF THE FIRST ADVERTS TO APPEAR IN ONE OF THE LOCAL PAPERS TELLING OF COMING MOVIES.

THE DEATH OF THOMAS ARBUCKLE

In the Marrowbone on the 4th of May
The dawn brought forth a tragic day
Young Arbuckle lying upon his bed
Little dreaming he would soon be dead

This youth a victim of fate was he
He joined the Army the world to see
But like many an Irish lad before
It wasn't long 'till his heart was sore

The Army lured him, the posters gay
So from his home he went away
What damned lies did the posters tell
For the Army meant a life of hell

At Easter time he came home on leave
His wife and home his heart did grieve
I'll not go back, he calmly said
And for this crime they shot him dead.

Tragedy did indeed come to the door of the Arbuckle family on May 4th 1937. Thomas Arbuckle was one of a family of nine whose home was at Mayfair Street in the Bone. In March 1936 Thomas Arbuckle joined the Royal Irish Fusiliers, an attempt no doubt to escape from the poverty at home and perhaps a happier and more prosperous life elsewhere. Many young men from the area followed the same road. Thomas Arbuckle was not so lucky. A twenty year old married man , he had been stationed at Borden Camp, Hants, England. He came back home on leave at Easter and on remaining he was posted as a deserter. Several weeks before his death he evaded capture by an R.U.C. man in Gracehill Street. The story told was that the policeman was left holding the man's coat by the collar while he made good his escape. Remaining in the Bone however proved to be a fatal mistake. Someone tipped off the R.U.C. where he was staying one night and the police along with military personnel from Victoria Barracks swiftly moved in to capture him. The raiding party came up the Oldpark Road into Ardilea Street at 5.40 a.m. Thomas Arbuckle was alerted by their noisy arrival and he quickly jumped over the back yard wall and ran down the side of the ' big field wall'. The raiding party consisted of 9 R.U.C. men accompanied by military police. When they entered Gilmore's house at 72a Ardilea Street, they soon realised that Thomas Arbuckle was escaping down the back. They immediately set off in hot pursuit. The police spotted him dashing across Ardilea Street to the entry which led out onto the 'Brickyard'. At this point an R.U.C. constable fired two shots at him. Thomas Arbuckle was seen to limp and stagger towards a lamp at the side of Highfield Mill, seriously wounded. On hearing the commotion, a crowd gathered and they immediately carried young Arbuckle into the mill where he received first aid while awaiting the arrival of the ambulance. He died at 12.45 p.m. in The Mater Hospital where surgeons fought to save his life. Several arteries had been severed and he had unfortunately lost too much blood. Arbuckle's needless death brought about more grief in the parish. Many asked the question; why did this young man have to be killed? The Government promised an immediate inquiry.

SHOT WHILE TRYING TO ESCAPE

Army Absentee Dies In Mater Hospital

TRAGIC AFFAIR IN BELFAST

Question In Northern House Of Commons

A 20-year-old Belfast youth who ... absentee from the Royal Irish Fusiliers was fatall... in the Old-park Road area of Belfast, w... ...ted to escape from the police

He was Thomas Arbuckle, of 27... ...ld.

He joined the Royal Irish Fusi... ...and had been stationed at Bord... He came to Belfast on leave ... was posted as a deserter.

At about 5-40 yesterday m... ...Ardilea Street, where he had be... ...t, when policemen—nine in nu... ...e accompanied by military pol... ...the door being opened they ma... ...er portion of the premises.

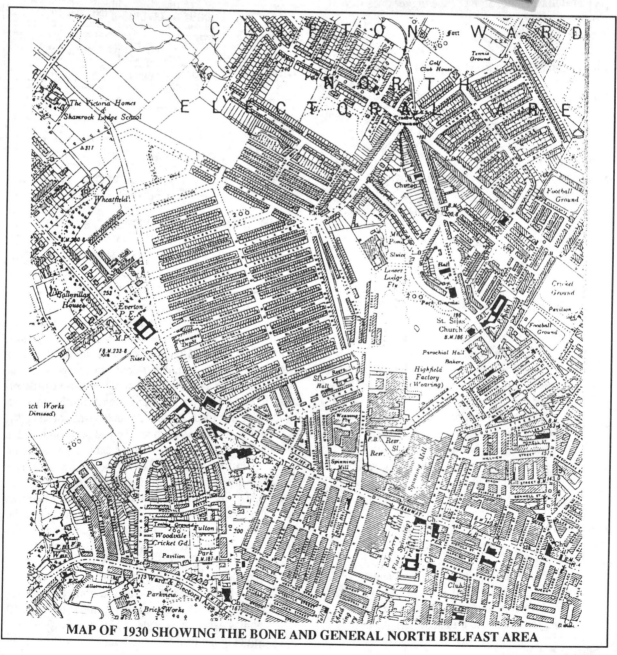

MAP OF 1930 SHOWING THE BONE AND GENERAL NORTH BELFAST AREA

DEVASTATION AT WALTON STREET

St. SILA'S PARISH CHURCH, OLDPARK ROAD, WHICH RECEIVED A DIRECT HIT IN THE LUFTWAFFE BLITZ
(THIS CHURCH WAS LOCATED AT THE JUNCTION OF ARDOYNE AVENUE AND OLDPARK ROAD.)

BALLYCARRY STREET AFTER THE DEVASTATION CAUSED BY THE GERMAN LUFTWAFFE IN 1941

slept rough under hedges and in barns. The overall death toll from the raids was over 1,000 lives lost. 2,500 people were injured and 56,000 houses were wrecked.

MAN SALVAGING HIS BOOK COLLECTION FROM HIS HOUSE AT ROSELEIGH STREET

The clear-up operation was a huge task. The dam at Wallace's Brickyard was selected as an infill site for the rubble from the wrecked buildings. Since most of the rubble from the Jubilee Hospital was dumped there the place was nicknamed 'The Jubilee Hills'. They are now known as the Bone Hills. Some rubble from Gallagher's Cigarette Factory was dumped there and children from the area used to dig for tobacco itself which was among the rubble. The sites at Ballynure Street, Ballyclare Street, and Sylvan Street were eventually replaced with new houses and flats. The site at Gracehill Street was cleared and remained as vacant ground until the recent housing development in the 1980's. The site of St. Sila's Church was cleared and a garage was built there in 1958.

Several people from the Bone were decorated for their bravery in The Second World War. 'Taffy' Evans from Gracehill Street won a Military Medal. John Collins from Ardilea Street won a Navy Cross to name but a few .

The following is a list of the dead taken from mortuary documents of the time;

John Mc Erlean.............................Glenview Street
Miss R.E. Murray..........................89 Gracehill Street
Margaret Murray...........................89 Gracehill Street
Catherine McCaffery............... ...85 Gracehill Street
Alexander Crothers........................23 Louisa Street
Sarah McFall.................................33 Louisa Street
Joseph McFall...............................33 Louisa Street
Joseph McFall (Jnr.)......................33 Louisa Street
Martha Reid..................................33 Louisa Street
John Lennon.................................32 Louisa Street
Catherine Hamilton......................18 Walton Street
Catherine Walsh...........................20 Walton Street
Annie English Brown....................22 Walton Street
Sarah Hillock...............................26 Sylvan Street
D. Mateer....................................28 Sylvan Street

F. Mateer.....................................28 Sylvan Street
Wm. Douglas ....8 Ballynure Street
Adam McAteer............................14 Ballynure Street
Martha McAteer..........................14 Ballynure Street
John Gray...................................18 Ballyclare Street
Sarah Gray.................................18 Ballyclare Street
Wm. McDowell ....20 Ballyclare Street
Audrey Skelton............................20 Ballycarry Street
Samuel Skelton...........................29 Ballycarry Street
S. Weldon...................................71 Ballycarry Street
Georgina Jackson.........................11 Ballymena Street
Thomas Jackson...........................11 Ballymena Street
Thomas Jackson (Jnr.)...................11 Ballymena Street
John Bell.....................................21 Ballymena Street

INDUSTRY IN THE BONE

The mills were central to life in the Bone as it was around the mills that this community grew. The area began when John Savage erected a mill in 1868. This mill complex was called Prospect Mills and was principally a flax spinning mill. It was later known as Lindsay Thompson's Mill. They specialised in flax spinning, thread manufacturing bleaching and dying.

Before Savage's Mill arrived, Wm. Ewart erected the Crumlin Road Flax Spinning Mill. This was by far the largest mill and the biggest employer in the immediate area. In fact this mill was at one time the largest flax mill in the entire world.

Beside the Prospect Mills was the Highfield Factory. This factory was principally a weaving factory. It was originally owned by James and Samuel Johnson. By 1950 Beltex Ltd. had taken it over to manufacture underwear.

Lower Lodge Factory specialised in both spinning and weaving. This complex was one of the oldest in the area. It initially housed a print-works and a cornmill until it was taken over by Messrs. Shaw Brown & Sons Ltd. as a spinning and weaving factory. It eventually housed, The Northern Bacon & Canning Factory and The Ulster Plastics Factory which were to become known as the Belmore Factories.

The Mourne Clothing Factory was opened in 1952 at Ardoyne Avenue. This factory closed when it was gutted by fire on Internment Night 1971.

With the advent of the mills came many new professions;

Beetler, Hacklesetter, Threadfinisher, Stitcher, Dyer, Weaver, Rougher, Bleacher, Flaxdresser, Spinning-Master, Scutcher, Linenlapper, Reeling-Master, Spinner, Bundler, Carding-Master, Hackler, Striker, and Doffer being a few of them.

Most people in the mills worked a full eleven hour shift every day with half day Saturday. There was no work on Sundays. Conditions in these Victorian Mills were abissmal with the result that many of the workers became susceptible to some of the most horrific diseases which developed in Belfast. The noise alone in these mills required people to constantly shout in order to be heard above the din.

WILLIAM EWART

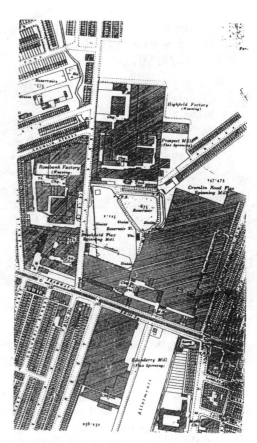

1940 MAP SHOWING THE LOCAL MILLS

Many children were put to work in the mills. At 10 years of age they would work as halftimers. One day at work and the next at school. At 12 years of age they became full timers from 6.30 a.m.. to 6.00 p.m. and 1.00 p.m. on Saturdays. It was in working conditions such as these that Jim Larkin and James Connolly tried to persuade the workers to organise themselves into unions. The days of the flax mills are now gone and today all we have remaining are the empty structures to remind us how hard our parents worked and toiled.

The Bone attracted several other businesses to the area over the years. The Irish Match Company opened a factory in 1895 at Ardilea Street. Here matches were made and boxed. Indeed many residents got part time employment which they could do at home, glueing the matchboxes. Wallace's Brick and Tile Manufacturers opened at Ardilea Street in 1880. It was with this factory that we have the emergence of the 'Brickyard' and Wallace's Dam. The factory used the clay from where the Bone hills are now to make the bricks.

Finally 1920 saw the opening of The City Bakery at 27-33 Ardilea Street. This was the site of the old Match Factory. With the bakery a stabling yard was opened behind Ardilea Drive, roughly where the new phase of houses are being built at Ardilea Street / Oldpark Road. Here Bob Kennedy and others were employed as blacksmiths. He shod the bakery horses and done other blacksmith's work for anyone else around the area. It was at this yard where one of the original wells was situated. The bakery was supplied

GLENVIEW ARMS

WEEKLY ENTERTAINMENT

TUESDAY'S

"WHEELS"

Play Your Cards Right
Prizes Galore

**HAPPY HOUR
9 - 10**

Pints & Vodka
£1.00

LATE BAR

THURSDAY

QUIZ NIGHT
In The Lounge

QUIZ MASTER

"FRA"

GREAT CRACK

LATE BAR

FRIDAY

BIG BANDS
"THE LOOK"

**ALSO COMING
ATTRACTIONS**

SUITE 2. C. U.
RASCALS
GA GA
T.P. BAND
DRUMS & WIRES
Dr. RAW

LATE BAR

SATURDAY AFTERNOONS

**SING SONG
IN LOUNGE**

SATURDAY NIGHT

"ENIGMA"
Plus Take Your Pick

LATE BAR

ALSO AVAILABLE FOR WEDDINGS

**FREE ROOM
FREE TOAST
FREE DISCO**

SPECIAL OFFERS
You Can't Beat
Our Menu Prices

**NOW TAKING BOOKINGS FOR
MOTHER'S DAY
ENTERTAINMENT INCLUDED**

ALSO AVAILABLE FOR
PRIVATE PARTIES
ANNIVERSARIES
OR ANY OTHER FUNCTIONS

TELEPHONE 745455

with horses by a man from Ardilea Street named Crossey. One thing that many people can recall about the bakery is getting a bag of clippings. When the delivery man came back with his horse and cart, there was a drawer under the cart. The purpose of this drawer was to catch all the bits of buns and cakes. Children used to go up to the bakery with a pillow case and the baker would fill it with bits of buns and icing. A bag of clippings cost sixpence.

It is an unfortunate reality but there are no industries in the Bone today.

Another job which was associated with the mills was the 'knocker-upper'. Although the term has several meanings now, in the days when the mills were active the knocker-upper had the job of knocking on people's doors to get them up early for work. There were several people from the Bone who had this job through the years. Among them was a Mrs. Topping from Mayfair Street.

Some people kept pigs and they fed them on scraps etc. which the residents in the area would leave at their back doors. These skins as they were called were gathered by youths from the area who had their own little business with the pig owners. More often than not it was the cause of many fights to establish who had the right to collect skins in certain entries in the Bone.

Bottles and jars were collected as glass was worth money. You could have used jars to get into the cinema. Rags were also collected and the 'ragman' used to walk around the streets every week pushing a cart collecting old unwanted clothes from householders.

OLD COTTAGE, THE LAST OF THE WELL KNOWN VILLAGE AT OLDPARK, HAVING ITS ROOF THATCHED IN 1938

PAWNS AND CHIP-SHOPS

One of the most memorable services in any area has to be the Pawn. Pawnbrokers were first listed in the Bone/Oldpark area in 1897. The principle pawnbrokers then were the Martin family.

R. Martin's Pawnshop
Oldpark Rd. at Ballymena Street
Robert Martin's Pawnshop
Oldpark Rd. between Shannon St. and Suir St.
Robert Martin's Pawnshop
40 Oldpark Rd. at Byron Street.
John Martin's Pawnshop
75 Mountview Street
John Martin's Pawnshop
99 / 101 Hillview Street
Walkers Pawnshop
Oldpark Road.
(Four doors above Finiston School.)
R.Tilley's Pawnshop
52 Oldpark Road.

All the above listed pawnshops were conducting business in the area in 1899. Before this Michael Kerr owned the first pawnshop on the Oldpark Road at the corner of Shannon Street. At one stage it was a thriving business but eventually only two pawnshops remained; Mitchell's at the corner of Oldpark Road and Ballymena Street and Davidson's at 33 /35 Oldpark Road (at Suir Street). Everyone made use of the pawn to borrow money on their valued possessions. Most families had their fathers good suit regularly kept in the pawnshop from Monday to Friday when it would be wrapped up in brown paper and given back to the owner when the loan was paid back. The pawnshops finally left the area in the 1970's.

Another public service available to the people of the Bone were the chip shops, or to give them their proper title, the Supper Salon. There were four of these establishments in the district.

Mrs. Jane Harper's at the corner of Oldpark Avenue.
The Earlscourt, 166 Oldpark Road (at Mayfair Street).
S. Bacci and Co. 351 / 353 Oldpark Road (opposite the playing pitches, known locally as Smokey Joe's).
Wm. Armstrong's at the corner of Glenpark St. and Louisa St.

Chippies flourished along with the advent of the cinema in Belfast. Harper's was the first such chip shop to arrive on the road, and it was a great meeting place for teenagers at the time before they went off to the pictures or the dances.

PUBS AND CLUBS

One of the first buildings to be established in the Bone was Brown's Public House at the end of Antigua Street. Then McAleavey's opened a spirit grocery store at the corner of Ardilea and Glenpark Streets. Armstrong's opened a pub at the corner of Oldpark Road and Ardilea Street. There were certainly plenty of places for the men of the area to get a drink, indeed there have been pubs in the area ever since.

Armstrong's became Peter O'Hare's and then finally was taken over by P.J. McKenna until it was bombed in the 1970's. P. Carroll's became Brigid Fearon's which later

Francies
Ardoyne Avenue

MONDAY

Quiz In The Lounge
£1.05 Pints & Vodkas

TUESDAY

Old Time Dancing In Cabaret
Bingo And Up To £1000 Snowball

WEDNESDAY

Quiz In Lounge
(Strarting Wednesday's in February)

THURSDAY

Cabaret (Available for bookings)
Buffets On Request

FRIDAY

Disco In Cabaret
The Best of House Techno & Garage

SATURDAY AFTERNOON

Folk In Lounge

SATURDAY NIGHT

Night Flight Disco
Group Every Second Week

became Gray's and finally is known today as The Park Inn and is situated at the corner of Lower Lodge Avenue (The Brae) and Oldpark Road.

McAleavey's became Farrell's. Then it was converted into a shop owned by J. Merniel. It eventually became The Catholic Ex-Servicemen's Club until it was demolished to make way for housing in the area.

Peter Connolly's Pub was at the bottom of Glenpark Street. It eventually became James Rocks' Pub until it too was demolished for housing redevelopment. Other pubs in the locality were:

James Jeffer's - 72 Oldpark Road (Byron Street)
F. McGovern's - 92 Oldpark Road (Hillview Street)
E. McGee's - 100/102 Hillview Street
E. McLean's - 59/61 Hillview Street
Hugh Rankin's - 31 Everton Street
Pat Woods' - 45 Louisa Street
(previously Owen McNeill's)
P.J. Campbell's - 1 Ballycarry St.
(Previously Catherine Murray's, the premises were eventually known as The Hole in the Wall)

As a result of the sustained violence, clubs were established as places of entertainment within the district. Most of the pubs had been bombed or closed because of intimidation. The clubs survived until the 1990's when many were forced out of business with the tightening of the licensing laws. There were three clubs in the Bone:

The Hole in the Wall....This club was initially located at Ballycarry Street then, it moved premises to the rear of Ardilea Street. The Catholic Ex-Servicemen's Club. This club was initially in Ardilea Street at the site of Merniel's Shop. It was also known as The Cassidy and Smith Memorial Hall. The club then moved premises to the vacant site of Ferguson's Shop on the Oldpark Road at the corner of Ballyclare Street.

The Glenpark. This club was originally at Rothsay Street. A new club was erected at Ardoyne Avenue/Oldpark Road.

Other clubs moved into the Bone when the Beltex factories became available as sites; The Shamrock Club and Ardoyne Kickham's G.A.A. The factories at the top of Havana Street were converted into a pub called The Jamaica Inn. The Glenpark was eventually forced to close but the site was eventually bought and reopened as a public House called Francie's.

An old club which was established in the Bone in the 1930's was The Prospect Club. This club was built in Saundersons Street out of material from the old League Hall which was then being dismantled. The club opened on St. Patrick's Day 1936. It had two billiard tables and a card room. The club also boasted a football team which played under the name Glendara. The caretakers were B. Collins and Pat Simpson. During The Second World War the premises were handed over to the parish priest and were used as the school meals centre.

Another club which was established in the area was The Sean McCaughey Club at Ardilea Street. It was run by republicans from the Bone such as Frank McGlade. Irish dancing and Irish Language classes were held there regularly. The club was opened in 1953 and was situated just where the entrance gates to St.Gemma's School are today. The club closed in 1966 to to clear the site for the building of this School.

SPORTS

One of the sports that attends to all working class areas, and the Bone is no exception, is that sport of kings- horse racing. Where so many strive for so long for so little; occasionally someone hits a jackpot. Some punters back horses, some back jockeys. Then there's the 'scud'. Who's the scud on your pitch? Canadians, Yankees, Accumulators, are just a few of the new fangled bets nowadays but did you know that the bookies shop as we know it, or to give them their proper title, the Turf Commission Agent, only became legal in 1957.

A Betting and Lotteries Act for Northern Ireland on the 29th of July 1957 was passed, "to provide for the regulation of Bookmakers and Bookmaking Offices; to make provision with respect to totalisators on horse race courses; to amend the law with respect to lotteries and special prize competitions; to permit ready money pool betting in certain circumstances; to abolish football betting duty; and for purposes connected with the matters aforesaid or any of them."

Certainly it was legal to have a bet at the racecourse but here in the Bone as well as in other areas throughout Belfast people ran 'books', all be it illegally. The first legal Bookies Shop to open in the Bone was Clark and Long's at Antigua Street, in what was originally Diamond's Pub.

Don't let us forget that other bygone sport which was played by many on the 'Brickyard' of Marrowbone, Pitch and Toss. Who can remember the peeler on the silver motorbike scattering upwards of 100 men at a time, as he drove into the middle of them, escaping with the pool? Pitch and Toss was a big money spinner and 'Durango' certainly took his share for the R.U.C. Benevolent Fund.

How many secret card-schools flourished or still flourish today? Then there are the Darts Clubs, Fishing Clubs, Golf Clubs and Bowling Clubs.

The best known soccer team was at one time called The Hearts and many's the battle they played on the 'Brickyard' and Flax Street pitches. Soccer was well catered for here and the matches on the Flax Street pitches attracted large crowds regularly. In the Parochial Hall boxing was promoted. The Sacred Heart Boxing Team was started in 1962 and was recognised in 1963. Their first coach was Gerry Smith and their first champion was J. Maguire.

Also prominent in the area are the pigeon men, greyhound men not to mention pony and trap. Then there are the

PARK INN

OLDPARK ROAD

*WECOMES YOU
TO
OUR POPULAR
LOUNGE BAR*

TUESDAY
QUIZ NIGHT

WEDNESDAY
DARTS NIGHT

FRIDAY
POP QUIZ

SATURDAY
FOLK NIGHT
AND
TAKE YOUR PICK

HAPPY HOURS EVERY SATURDAY UNTIL 2.00 P.M.

Ard Eoin C.L.G.

Traditional Home of 'Bone Gaels'

Would like to thank the people of the 'Bone' and Sacred Heart for their support over the years and look forward to more of the same in the future.

**TRAINING
EVERY
SUNDAY
6 TO 18 yrs.
ALL
WELCOME**

Ard Eoin Kickhams

**FOOTBALL
HURLING
CAMOGIE
DANCE
LANGUAGE
CULTURE**

CONGRATS!

A wonderful publication about a great place and a great people.

TWO FOOTBALL TEAMS FROM THE BONE AROUND 1950 AT THE FLAX STREET PITCH

billiards, snooker and pool teams. The Bone can match any other district for sports.

One of the most controversial titles to have is that of the 'hard man'. Who would claim to be the hardmen of the Bone today? Some of those who once held the title were The Ferrin brothers from Parkview Street. Kane, Kearney, Cassidy and of course Nailer Clarke. These were the people who ensured that no-one cheated at the Pitch and Toss or at the card schools.

SACRED HEART SCHOOL 1930

THE GLENVIEW STREET SCHOOL

Glenview Street was an important street in the Bone. It was here that all the local children attended school. It was here that they attended Mass.

Did you know that the school has had five different titles?

Antigua Street National School
Wm. Brown was the principle.

St. Patrick's National School
H. O'Donnell was principle. (1890 to 1895)

St. Macanisus' National School
Mr. Kerris and Mrs. McArdle were principles.
(1895 to 1921)

St. Columban's Public Elementary School
1921 to 1986.

Sacred Heart Primary School
New premises at Oldpark Avenue.

As has been stated earlier the school at Glenview Street were one of the best in the city and housed both boys and girls in segregated classes. This school eventually became overcrowded and in 1966 the girls moved from Glenview Street to a newly erected school at Deanby Gardens. This new school was called Our Lady's Girls School. The principle, Miss T. McManus, moved from Glenview Street to administrate the new school.

The Glenview Street Schools were eventually demolished and the school was relocated at the football pitch behind Oldpark Avenue. The new school was called Sacred Heart Primary. Set on more spacious grounds the new modern designed school opened in 1987.

SACRED HEART CHURCH

In the 1930's McGrath's Religious Reliquary Shop was in business opposite Sacred Heart Church gates in Glenview Street. They sold Rosary Beads, Mass cards, prayer books etc. Charlie Delaney owned a newsagents shop at the corner of the street. He also sold hurling sticks and sliotars. He eventually moved his business up onto the Crumlin Road above the Forum. Sacred Heart Church remained unchanged with it's impressive round tower until in 1967 major refurbishments at the church were undertaken. The St. Brigid's Tower was demolished to make a new entrance. The altar was also renovated and work was complete in 1968. Further renovations to the church grounds took place in 1986. A large extension and garage were added to the Presbetry in 1985/86.

SACRED HEART CHURCH. 1905

DID YOU KNOW ?

That electricity was introduced to the Bone and greater Oldpark area when the first tram lines were put on the Oldpark Road in 1913. Even though it was available since then, the majority of people used gas lamps and candles until the 1940's.

Mitchell's pawn shop was originally in Ardilea Street untill it was burnt in the 1920s riots.

That the fare from City Hall to the Sacred Heart Chapel on the tram was 3d. (Thrupence or three old pennies)

That the first person to own a Rolls Royce in the Bone was, Mary Ann Skelly from Gracehill Street.

That the first Sinn Fein councillor for Ardoyne and the Bone was, Michael Carolan, a school teacher from Chief Street.

That people used to buy hay in Ferguson's Shop at the corner of Oldpark Road and Ballyclare Street to make mattresses.

That at one stage there were three chemist shops on the Oldpark Road at the Bone; Watterson's at 157 Oldpark Road, McKee's at 167 Oldpark Road, and City Chemists at 176 Oldpark Road, at the corner of Gracehill Street.

GHOST STORIES FROM THE BONE

Many chilling ghost stories and tales of supernatural happenings have been told down through the years and the Bone has had it's own tales to tell.

One of Belfast's most famous ghosts is that of Galloper Thompson. This was allegedly the son of the local mill-owner, Lindsay Thompson. Thompson's Prospect Mill was one of the bigger Belfast flax spinning mills and it stretched between Flax Street and Ardilea Street. His son apparently told his friends that if he didn't get into heaven when he died he would come back and haunt the area where he died and so the stories of sightings around the Bone abound. Apparently he could be seen racing at speed on a white horse after dark. Some people claimed that he had no head but others discounted this claiming that because he was racing so fast he was stooped over on his horse and so he only appeared to be headless. Many parents in the area still tell their children that if they don't come indoors early for school the next morning, then Galloper Thompson would catch them and take them away. Stories and sightings of the horseman have all but ceased now however. The reason given was that an intrepid ghost catcher tricked Galloper Thompson and he managed to imprison the ghost in a whiskey bottle which he corked and threw into the outgoing tide at Belfast Lough. Perhaps poor Galloper Thompson is tonight racing around the streets of Liverpool trying to get back to his beloved Belfast.

Another intriguing story is that of the ghost who haunts the grounds behind the Jamaica Inn. The ghost of a British soldier apparently roams the area both day and night. It is said that he died when a German bomb claimed a direct hit on the gun position he was manning on the night of the Belfast Blitz. Indeed the wreckage of the shelter is still there today.

Another story from the Belmore Factories at Havana Street is that one night while the watchman was sitting reading at a table in his room he felt an eerie feeling come over him as though someone was watching him. As he raised his eyes from his book, he froze in horror. There, standing in front of him in the doorway were an elderly couple, smiling

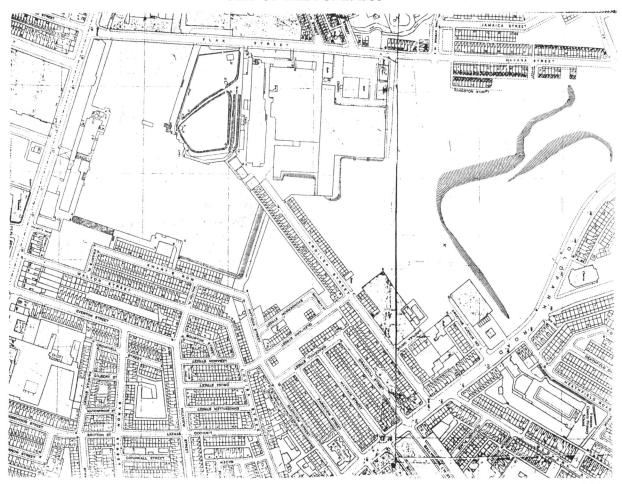

at him. They never spoke a word and remained in the doorway for what seemed like an age before disappearing. The terrified watchman fled, never to return.

The Banshee has also allegedly been sighted in the area many times. Her screams have been compared to the crying of a large cat mixed with the wailing of a woman in deep sorrow. Her cry always announces someone's death. However she only follows those families which begin with 'O' or 'Mac' and is native to every area in Ireland. Tales of the banshee originate at the time of Fionn Mac Cool and Cu-Chulainn, when she followed her warrior heroes to the battlefield, wailing both in fear and encouragement. When they died she shrieked in sorrow as though her own soul had been pierced. The banshee takes the form of a wizened old woman. She stands about four feet tall, miserably thin, with long silver-grey hair streaming to the ground and wears a long white dress. It is said that she sits on the wall of the house of the person who is about to die, combing her long hair while wailing and shrieking in deep sorrow. Next time you think you hear cats screeching during the night, think twice.

There has been persistent talk about the 'Green Lady' who haunted the 'Brickyard'. This area has since been redeveloped and now has been replaced with a maze of little streets from the Flax Centre to Francie's Public House at the top of Ardoyne Avenue. For years people wouldn't cross the 'Brickyard' after dark for fear of bumping into 'The Green Lady'.

The following story is by far the scariest one of all. The horrific story of 'Johnny the Bomb Thrower' has been told through the years and after much research, I finally discovered the complete story of this ghost who still haunts the Bone. Many people claimed to have seen this ghost in Gracehill Street or roaming the area around the big field wall behind Saundersons Street. The story starts at the height of the troubles in the 1920's when Johnny threw a bomb into the midst of a group of children who were playing in Gracehill Street. British soldiers from the Norfolk Regiment who were stationed in the area at the time gave chase and caught him. A hostile crowd soon gathered and the military handed him over to the men from the Bone and he was never seen alive again. Locals identified the bomber as a man from Beresford Street, in the Shankill called Johnny Lusty. He was apparently beaten to death and his body was dumped over the 'fieldy wall'. Later that same night his corpse was buried on the 'Brickyard' in a lime filled grave somewhere about where Jamaica Road meets Ardoyne Avenue. For years since his death, a walk along Ardoyne Avenue late at night sends a shiver down even the hardest man's spine. The story continues today that Johnny haunts the area around Rothsay, Saunderson and Antigua Streets. His appearance is always heralded by children's voices singing, "In and out goes dusty bluebells, I'll be your master."

MAHONEY'S ROW

(The following is based on a newspaper report published

at the time of the demolition of Ardilea Street)

A microcosm of nineteenth century Belfast in the Oldpark area of the city has disappeared under the weight of bulldozers. It was a simple row of eight 100-year old terraced houses at Ardilea Street. They had been inhabited by the Mahoney family only and was known as 'Mahoney's Row.'

The Mahoney's and their relations had lived in the houses for six generations and as the era of redevelopment drew nearer, the last remaining family reluctantly packed up and left. Forty three year old Joseph Saunders, whose mother was a Mahoney, lived in the house all his life and did not want to leave it. "It was part of me and my family. The houses were in bad condition but it was the whole atmosphere - there was a history as long as your arm for my house alone. I had thought of putting up a protest, but it would have done no good; if they're going to build, they'll build." he said.

His love for Mahoney's Row was supported by many other Mahoney's and indeed by many residents of the Oldpark, more commonly known as " The Bone."

The houses were built before before the Boer War in 1899 by a local Brick company for it's workers. There was waste land on both sides so that the houses made a complete unit. There were no machines in those days, so the bricks had to be hand-made, that's one special feature of the houses.

When the brick factory closed down, a bakery company took over and the men kept their houses . They were eventually taken over by The Housing Executive.

Outside one of the houses before the demolition began, was a huge stone block, which at one time was obviously a white colour, turned greyish black. There used to be one outside every door. Their use was simple. During the summer the men would all come outside and talk, and they'd sit on the stones. They were all from the brickyard. The last stone has been weathered away by wind and rain."The day I took my leave, and said my final farewell to Mahoney's Row was one of the saddest days in my whole life I did not want to let go", said Mr. Joe Saunders, a resident of the old street. My house was an heirloom, part of my family's heritage. The small inconspicuous row of terrace houses was one of the finest examples of working class life in Belfast at the turn of the century, " he said, "Now it's gone."

Mahoney is only one of the surnames one associates with the Bone. Some others would be, Mc Nally, Owens, Mulholland, Kane, Doherty, Molloy, Cassidy, Brown, Barnes, Ferrin, and Markey. A quick glance at the street directories in this booklet will show how many names are native to the Bone and just how many of those are still here today. Many of the residents of the district are inter-related and someone once said "if you throw a stone in the Bone you're bound to hit someone belonging to you." It has always been a close-knit community. This has been because of the hardship they have endured throughout the years and in fact still endure today. A working-class community that anyone would feel proud to be part of.

THE LODGE WHICH WAS REPLACED BY ROSAPENNA STREET.
THIS LODGE BECAME KNOWN AS THE 'NEW LODGE' . THE ROAD LEADING TO THIS HOUSE
WAS KNOWN AS THE NEW LODGE ROAD AND THE UPPER SECTION LATER BECAME KNOWN
AS THE CLIFTONVILLE ROAD

THE GROWTH OF THE BONE/MARROWBONE

1790.......Robert Howie's Bleach Green established.

1800.......Oldpark Linen Bleach Mill listed.

1824.......McPherson's Cotton Printworks established.

1847.......Potato blight. Millions die or flee their homes.

1867.......The Fenian Rising.

1868.......Savage's Row and Savage's Mill established.

1869.......Catholic Church opened at Ardoyne.

1880.......Savage's Row becomes Ardilea Street. Rothsay St., Glenpark St., Antigua St., and Saunderson Street built in the immediate vicinity. Wallace's Brickworks established at Ardilea Street.

1887......Gracehill St., Mayfair St., and Parkview St. were built. Oldpark Road was developed up as far as Ardilea Street on one side and as far as Oldpark Avenue on the other side.

1889......Sacred Heart Church and Presbetry opened.

1890......Finiston School listed. The rest of The Bone's streets completed.

1895......'Bally' Streets built. Irish Match Company opens next to Wallace's Brickworks in Ardilea Street.

1899......Oldpark farmyard listed. Finiston Post Office first appears on the Oldpark Road.

1900......Havana Street, Kingston Street, and Ardoyne Avenue are built. St. Sila's Church is listed as being located at Oldpark Farmyard.

1902......Holy Cross new Church opens at Ardoyne. St. Sila's new Church opens at the corner of Ardoyne Avenue and Oldpark Road.

1906.....Belfast Free Public Library opens on the Oldpark Road at Century Street.

1914.....First World War breaks out.

1916.....Easter Rebellion in Dublin.

1920.....Beginning of serious troubles in Belfast. City Bakery opens at Ardilea Street.

1921......Glenview Street Schools built.

1922......Partition of Ireland. Antigua Street, Rothsay Street and Saunderson Street destroyed in sectarian violence.

1924......Parochial Hall built. Gracehill Street (The New Street) built.

1929......Wall Street Crash, World Depression.

1932......Outdoor Relief Riots. Curfew imposed. Rioting in the Bone and Oldpark areas.

1935......Torrens Avenue built completing Heathfield / Torrens area.

1936.......Prospect Club opened at Saunderson Street. Park Cinema opens in December.

1937.......The death of Thomas Arbuckle.

1939.......Outbreak of The Second World War.

1941......R.U.C. Station opened at Torrens Avenue;
J.J. Shea Head Constable.
Germans bomb Belfast.

1945......Second World War ends.

1952.......Mourne Clothing Factory opens at Ardoyne Avenue.

1958.......Park Filling Station opens on Oldpark Road.

1966.......Oldpark Playing Pitches opened. Glenview Street Girls School closes and Deanby Gardens School opens.

1967.......Oldpark Pavilion and Park opened. St. Gemma's Secondary School for Girls opens at Ardilea Street.

1969........ Outbreak of present conflict.

1980 ....Beginning of Redevelopment.

The following are extracts from the Belfast Street Directory for 1887

COMO TERRACE.
1 Richardson, J. A., vandriver
2 Millsop, Mrs. Margaret
3 Vacant
4 Steer, Geo., linenlapper
5 Johnston, Mrs. Jane
6 Dowson, Thos., yarn bundler
7 Hamilton, James, flaxdresser
8 Vacant
9 Patterson, James, tenter
10 M'Connell, John, block prntr

OLDPARK CRESCENT.
22 M'Bride, Robert, chandler
24 Lewis, Abraham, factory manager Northern Spin. Co.
26 M'Clung, John
28 Gray, Wm. M, factory mngr. Agnes St. Weaving Co.
30 Wilson, Frederick, miller, Glenwood flour mills
32 Vacant
......Benvell street intersects......

OLDPARK COTTAGE.
38 Williamson, John, flaxbuyer
40 Hamilton, James, do.
......Byron street intersects......

OLDPARK TERRACE.
42 Side door
44 Coates, Richard, manager Oldpark Bleach Works
46 Leitch, Charles N., flax mer.
48 Morrison, Edward, engineer
50 & 52 BEECHPARK NATIONAL SCHOOL — William Scilly, principal, teacher
56 Shaw, James
58 & 60 M'Gurk, Mary, publcn.
......Hillview street intersects......

VERNANT LODGE.
Hunter, S. O., manager Wm. Ewart & Sons, Ld., Crumlin road
......Louisa street intersects......

RUSHFIELD.
90 M'Cann, M., superannuated officer, I.R.
92 Pinkerton, David, rent agent
94 Stewart, James, bookkeeper
96 Mills, Martha
......Parkview street intersects......

MAYFORE COTTAGES.
122 Vacant
124 Larkin, Henry, flaxdresser
126 Smylie, William, gardener
128 Morton, Andw, bread server
130 Steele, Samuel, labourer
132 Harris, Wm., reeling master
......Mayfore street intersects......

RUBY TERRACE.
134 M'Cartney, George, grocer
136 Mays, Wm. J., salesman
138 Shaw, George, clerk
140 Shaw, Robert, stonecutter
142 Vacant
144 Porter, James, clerk
......Gracehill street intersects......
152 Stevenson, Jas., upholsterer
154 Armstrong, John, publican
......Ardilea street intersects......

CAVE VIEW.
156 & 158 M'Kee, J. A., grocer
160 M'Caugherty, J., labourer
162 Collins, Robert, draper

OLDPARK AVENUE.
Off Oldpark road
1 O'Boyle, Mary, dairykeeper
3 Goudy, Robert, blockprinter
5 Bowman, John, teacher
7 Mathews, R. H., linenlapper
9 Martin, Henry, warehouse salesman
11 Miller, Margaret, weaver
...Oldpark place intersects...

GENEVA TERRACE.
13 Vacant
15 Adair, Mrs. Susan
17 Calwell, John, fitter
19 Johnston, James, carpenter
21 Rushton, Samuel, foreman moulder
23 Johnston, Wm., carpenter
25 Green, Francis, potato mer
New houses in course of erec
M'Cormick, Wm. J., professor in St. Malachy's Col

OLDPARK PLACE.
Off Oldpark avenue
2 Johnston, A., blockprinter
4 Carson, David, traveller
6 Curran, Francis, stonemason
8 Munroe, James, blockprinter
10 Simpson, Robert, tenter
12 Gallaher, Jas., blockprinter
14 Vacant
16 Steele, James, vandriver
18 Freeman, Wm., flaxdresser
20 Ferris, Wm. E., harbour con
22 M'Farlane, D., blockprinter
24 Hickland, James

OLDPARK HOUSE
Kernaghan, Hry, pointsman N. C. R.

36

ARDILEA STREET.
Off Oldpark Road

1 Arbuckles, Joseph, labourer
3 Donaghy, Jas., enginedriver

Oldpark Brickworks—Wallace, James, brick manufacturer
35 Hughes, Patrick, flaxdresser
37 Thomas, W., brickmoulder
39 Towman, Denis, labourer
41 M'Aleer, James, labourer
43 Haveron, Wm., labourer
45 M'Loughlin, P., labourer
47 M'Grath, Hugh, labourer
49 Maguire, Patrick, labourer
61 Goudy, S., flaxdresser
63 Vacant
65 Garrity, E., woodturner
67 Tumelty, T., flaxdresser
69 Donaghy, Agnes
71 M'Caffrey, John, carpenter
73 Rice, Bernard, labourer
75 M'Master, Elizabeth
77 M'Nally, Wm., flaxdresser
79 Devlin, Rose
81 Smith, John, labourer
83 Clarke, P., flaxdresser
85 O'Halloran, T., flaxdresser
87 Doyle, David, flaxdresser
89 Turley, Robt., flaxdresser
91 Vacant
93 Doyle, Mary, millworker
95 Orr, John, traveller
97 Douglas, Patrick, seaman
99 M'Loughlin, J., millworker
101 Shiels, Edwd., flaxdresser

103 M'Burney, W., millworker
105 Mulloy, E., flaxdresser
107 Gribbon, Thomas, labourer
109 Shields, John, carpenter
111 Vacant
113 Canter, Joseph, clerk
115 M'Grogan, M., millworker
117 Hinton, James, flaxdresser
2 Milliken, Samuel, grocer
4 Reid, Hugh, waiter
6 Larkin, Wm., labourer
8 M'Kee, Joseph, gardener
10 Hanna, Thos., flaxdresser
12 Peueli, T. M., draughtsman
14 M'Farlane, J., blockprinter
16 Hanna, Robert, labourer
18 Nugent, Mary, millworker
20 M'Gowan, T., blacksmith
22 Kearney, T., brickmoulder
24 Clarke, P., labourer
26 M'Nally, John, labourer
28 M'Clelland, Andw., carter
30 Clarke, Patrick, labourer
32 Griffin, Susan
34 Barr, James, flaxdresser
36 M'Kee, Joseph, labourer
38 to 42 Vacant
..... Glenpark st intersects ......
52 & 54 M'Aleavey, J., spirit grocer
56 Alexander, M. E., millwker
58 Vallely, A., flaxdresser
60 M'Kay, John, stationer
62 Needy, Wm., dairyman
64 M'Donnell, M., labourer
66 Waring, T., thread finisher

68 Davison, David, flaxdresser
70 Doran, John, flax dresser
72 Finnigan, Wm., labourer
74 Hughes, E., millworker
76 & 78 Vacant
80 Hughes, Edwd., flaxdresser
82 M'Quidy, Elizabeth
84 to 92 Vacant
94 Rooney, James, flaxdresser
96 M'Guiggan, D., flaxdresser
98 Mann, Denis, dyer
100 & 102 Vacant
104 Brennen, W., flaxdresser
106 to 110 Vacant
112 Barr, John, flaxdresser
114 M'Guiggan, P., flaxdresser
116 Donaghy, James, clerk
118 Vacant
120 M'Grogan, Jas., flaxdresser
122 & 124 Vacant
126 Shields, E., carpenter
128 M'Laughlin, H., flaxdresser
180 M'Clintock, A., enginedriver
132 Steed, James

PARKVIEW STREET.
Off Oldpark road.

1 Wilson, John, stonecutter
3 M'Veigh, George, coachman
5 Clayton, Isaac, labourer
7 Vacant
9 Hogan, Timothy, stonecutter
11 Fullen, Mrs. Mary
13 Earley, Patrick, carpenter

GLENPARK STREET.
Louisa street to Ard¹

A number of small houses

GRACEHILL STREET.
Off Oldpark road

2 Graham, Rose
4 Brown, James, tenter
6 Dick, James, clerk
8 Dickey, W., machine-master
10 Rainey, Mrs. Elizabeth
12 Neilly, James, ship's fireman
14 Vacant

ANTIGUA STREET.
Off Glenpark street.

1 Side door to 2 Glenpark st.
... Sanderson street intersects ...
3 Vacant
5 Vacant
7 Poland, John, tailor
9 Vacant
11 Weldon, Robert, brick manufacturer
2 & 4 Toner, John, grocer
6 Hill, Mary Ann
8 Gray, Nathaniel, driller
10 Rodgers, James, labourer
12 Murray, Jas., yarn bundler
14 M'Ildoon, H., engine driver
16 M'Cullough, P., flaxdresser
18 Travers, James, flaxdresser
20 Carson, John, labourer
22 Young, Mrs. L., millworker
24 Alexander, David, labourer
26 Gilmour, Mary Jane, weaver
28 & 30 ANTIGUA St NATIONAL

SAUNDERSON STREET

A number of small houses

OLDPARK ROAD.
Crumlin road to Ballysillan road

1 Williams, Wm., flesher
3 Ginger, John, com. traveller
5 Houston, George, flesher
7 Trimble, Annie, boot and shoe dealer
9 Morrow, Robert, grocer
......Foyle street intersects.......
11 Thompson, J. N., Northern Bakery
13 Munce, James, flesher
15 Wiseman, W. H., bootmaker
17 Bailey, John, shipwright
...... Bann street intersects ......
19 Bruce, James, grocer
MOUNT OLIVET.
21 M'Keown, Alex., mechanic
.....Shannon street intersects.....
M'DOWELL'S PLACE.
23 Kerr, Michael, pawnbroker
25 Ireland, J. M., confectioner
27 Pratt, T., bootmaker, &c.
.... Suir street intersects........
29 Robinson, David, grocer
MOUNT NEBO.
29A Vacant
31 O'Neill, J. B., bookkeeper
33 Trimble, Eliza, schl. teacher
35 Carrothers, Mary
PARK LODGE.
Dobbin, Wm., J.P. (of Wm. Dobbin & Co., Limited)
Dobbin, W. C., pharmaceutical chemist (of W. Dobbin & Co., Limited)

ROWELLAN.
Clarke, Rev. R. J., incumbent of Trinity Church
BENWELL TERRACE.
61 Weir, Richardson, draper
63 Barr, David, bookkeeper
65 Vacant
67 Adams, Ann J.
69 Jennings, Hugh, sch'l teachr
71 Hill, Geo. L, engraver
73 M'Clung, Sarah, draper
75 Campbell, James, grocer
......Beechpark st intersects......
BEECHPARK TERRACE.
77 Campbell, J., linenlapper
79 White, A., bandmaster
81 Mitchell, Robt. A., tenter
83 Porter, W. J., ship fireman
85 Mulholland, H., fireman
87 Wallace, T., commissn agent
89 Mairs, Mrs Sarah
91 Gamble, Mrs. Agnes
93 D'Courcey, E., bookkeeper
95 Livingstone, R. J., traveller
97 Brown, G., block printer
99 Gilchrist, W., flax buyer
101 M'Murray, Wm., traveller
103 Boyd, J., commission agent
105 Davidson, T., joiner
107 M'Clure, J., bricklayer
109 Robinson, J., carter

OLIVE TERRACE.
1 Campbell, Thos. J., labourer
2 Balmer, S., thread finisher
3 Gilmour, Wm., labourer
4 Stevenson, Wm., tenter
5 Campbell, Mrs. Jane
6 M'Leod, John, blockprinter
7 Simpson, David, painter
8 Boyd, Mrs. Elizabeth
9 Beggs, Wm., fireman
10 Gourley, Miss Mary

... Oldpark avenue intersects. ...

The following are extracts from the Belfast Street Directory for 1935

Oldpark Road

CRUMLIN RD. TO BALLYSILLAN ROAD.

1 Enfield Dairy Co.
3 M'Clelland, Chas., tobacconist and confctnr.
5 Oldpark Road Post Office —Margaret M'Clintock sub-postmistress
7 Devonshire laundry
,, Pearl Dye works
7a Orr, John
9 Dickson, Robt., fishmongr
11 Shepherd's Dairies, Ltd
13 Courtney, J., butcher
........Foyle st intersects.......
15 Thompson, W. M., bakery
17 Thompson, Miss E., drpr
19 O'Neill, Dominick, cnftnr
21 Moore, Thos., fruiterer
........Bann st intersects.........
23 M'Pherson, G., fish saloon
25 COMPTON, SAMUEL, Radio Dealer and News agent
......Shannon st intersects.....
27 Smyth, R. J., butcher
29 Kelso, Jas., confectioner
31 Strong, R., bootmaker
.. ..Suir st intersects.........
33, 35 Davison, W., pawnbkr
37 Shanks, M. E., hardware
39 Harrison, Elizabeth, confectionery and tobnst.
41 Clinton, S., draper

43 Rostofsky, B., tailor
45 Crowe, Wm., draper
47 Campbell, M., fruiterer
49 Hume, Wm., newsagt.
51 Armstrong, G., com. agt.
53 York, Sarah, draper
55 Ebenezer Gospel Hall
57 Dickson, W., draper
59 Hamilton, J., tobaccnst.
........Manor st intersects......
61 Noble's, boot repairing
61a Reilly, Miss Annie
63 Clements, John, flesher
65 Vacant
67 Bell, Mrs. Sarah
69 Adjey, W. J., linenlapper
71 Neville, John, labourer
73 Lyness, George
73a Richards, Wm., grocer
75 Mountford, E., manager
77 Foster, W. J.
79 Graham, Robt., draper
81 Lyttle, Mrs. Margaret
83 Silverman, Isaac, tailor
85 Cummins, Rchd., plater
87 Justice, R., plater
89 David, Ralph E., civ. svt.
91 Johnston, Mrs. Martha
93 Auld, Saml., engineer
95 Parkes, Mrs. Elizabeth
97 Sheridan, Chas. E., boat builder
99 Graham, W., breadserver
101 M'Ilveen, R., reelingmstr
103 Wolfson, Nathan, travlr.
105 Royal Laundry

105a Elliott, Mrs. E.
......Manor drive intersects ...
107 M'Greevy, H., R.U.C.
109 Parkes, Mrs. Annie
111 Whiteside, Mrs. R., drpr
113 Campbell, Miss Mary, midwife
115 Stewart, Mrs. Mary
117, 117a Dougan, A. M., pharmaceutical chemist
119 In course of re-construction
121 M'Clelland Bros., draprs
121a Curry, W. J., labr.
......Beechpark st intersects......
123 Graham, Robt., driver
125 M'Intyre, David, fitter
127 Hamilton, F., damask mounter
129 M'Neilly, John, checker
131 Tannahill, W., nwsagt.
133 M'Bride, Miss Sarah
135 Stewart, Mrs. A., boot merchant
137 Hewitt, A., fruiterer
139 MARTIN, THOMAS, Painter and Decorator
141 M'Grath, Mrs. Ellen
143 Boyle, Wm., tobacconist
145 Nevin & Co., fishmngrs.
147 M'Grath, J., hairdresser
149 Dickey, B., dairy
151 Gaston, Miss Rebecca
153 M'Kee, Wm., boilermkr.
155 Murray, C., grocer

......Mountview st intersects...
EWING, SAMUEL & SONS LTD., Mountview Building Works. 'Phone 1001.
157 Watterson, R. J., pharmaceutical chemist
159 Watterson, R. J., grocer
161 Rooney, Jas., butcher
163, 165 M'DOWELL, STEPHEN, Tobacconist, Confectioner and Fruiterer
167 M'Kee, W. J., chemist
169 Morris, Miss F., beauty parlour
171 Finiston Sub - Post Office—A. Davison, sub-postmaster
173 Kilpatrick, D., upholstr.
...Ballymoney st intersects. .
175 Braden, Mrs. Dorothy
177 Weir, Jas., caulker
179 Loughrine, Catherine
181 Gowdy, Saml., flaxdrssr
183 Kernaghan, F., painter
185 Fleming, Sarah, butcher
.....Ballymena st intersects. .
187, 189 Mitchell, E., pawnbroker
191 M'Grand, James, newsagent and tobacconist

2 Andrew's Medical Hall —goods entrance
10 Lemon, A.—side entrance
12 Gateway
14 Livingston, D., wallpaper merchants
16-18 Ulster Bank (Crumlin Road Branch)
20 Richardson, H. R., dentist
22-24 Smyth, R. J., butcher
26-28 Davison, Jos., dealer
30 Holiness Movement Ch.
32 M'Millan, Rev. W. A.
34 Graham, Hamilton, btchr.
36 Boyd, J., bootmaker
38 Watson, Miss Elizabeth
40 Salvation Army Hall
.......*Century st intersects*......
42-44 Vacant ground
46 BELFAST PUBLIC LIBRARY — No. 1 Carnegie Branch—A. E. Atkinson, branch librn.
48-52 Vacant ground
54 Simms, Rev. S., minister
56 Hillis, W., fishmonger
58 Whyte, Hugh, breadsvr.
60-64 CHURCH ARMY WORK AID AND LODGING HOUSE. Firewood Dealers—Capt. A. Ackroyd, Officer in Charge. Telephone: Belfast 2873
.....*Benwell st intersects*.....
38 Oldpark Radio Store
70 Oldpark Garage

... .*Byron st intersects*... ..
72 Farrell, C., spirit vaults
74 M'Carthy, P. J., B.A.
76 Gordon, Robert, clerk
78 Park, W. H., plant mngr.
80 North Belfast Christian Workers' Union
82 M'Govern, Eliza., cnftnr.
84-88 Graham, Wm. H., house furnisher
90 O'Kenny, Mrs. Rose
92 M'Govern, F., spt. mrcht.
.....*Hillview st intersects*......
94 M'Causland, S. A., grocer
96 Kirkwood, Jas., fitter
98 Henry, Mrs. E.
100 Law, Mrs.
102 Law, Susan, draper
...*Baden-Powell st intersects*...
104 Lynn Memorial Methodist Church — Minister, Rev. J. B. Ewens, The Manse, 310 Antrim road
106 Montgomery, Shaw, provision merchant
108 Newell, Benj., ins. agent
110 Vacant
110a Boyd & Co., printers
,, Cummings, J. A., furniture manufacturer
,, M'Crum, T. J., engineer
.....*Buller st intersects*......
112 Sunbeam Dairy Co.
114 Jeanette's, drapers
116 Cowan Bros., pastry bakers (branch)

118 Kirkwood, J. W., btchr.
120 M'Causland, M., statnr.
122 Dickson, R., fishmonger
124 Hassard, W. J., drprs.
.......*Louisa st intersects*......
126 to 132 Belfast Co-operative Society, Ltd.
134 Hyland, Dr. A.
136 Mulligan, R., assur. agt.
138 M'KEE, JAMES, dentist
140 Donaghy, R. J., clerk
142 Swann, H., stock-keeper
144 M'Cabe, J., barman
146 Tiernan, Patk., foreman
148 M'Guinness, Jas., grdnr.
150 Vacant
....*Glenview st intersects*
Sacred Heart Roman Catholic Chapel — Rev. John M'Auley, P.P.; Rev. J. Connor, C.C.; Rev. L. M'Keown, B.A., C.C.
......*Parkview st intersects*......
152 Smyth, Ed., coal mrcht.
154 Fanning, Jas., labourer
156 Hull, James, baker
158 Jack, Alex., labourer
160 Quinlon, Andw., labr.
162 Convery, B., travlr.
......*Mayfair st intersects*.....
164 Rooney, Wm., flesher
166 Herald, J., shoemaker
168 Kelly, Mrs. Rose
170 Noble, John, labourer
172 Shannon, J., engineer
174 Devlin, Patk., dealer

......*Gracehill st intersects*. ...
176 Maguire, Andw., fruitr.
178 Rooney, J., butcher
180 M'Keown, Arthur, dealer
182-184 O'Hare, P., publn.
......*Ardilea st intersects*.. ...
186 M'Kee Bros., grocers
188 Wallace, Jas., clerk
190 Kidd, Wm., plumber
192 Martin, T., tobacconist
194 Dawson, Mrs. M.
196 Aicken, John, glazier
198 Gillespie, Mrs. Roseanna
200 Todd, Wm., joiner
202 Savage, Henry, joiner
204 to 208 Caldwell, H., bldr.
210 Caldwell, Mrs. J.
212 Brown, Mrs.
214 Crowthers, Jas., engr.
216 Moore, William
218 Moore, Wm., linenlppr.
220 Cowan, Graham, insptr.
Ardoyne avenue intersects
222 St. Silas' Church— Rector, Rev. F. W. W. Warren, B.D.
224 to 334 Vacant ground
...*Lower Lodge av intersects*...
336 Fearon, Bridget, spirit merchant
338 Hutchinson, John, labr.
340 Thompson, Jas., joiner
342 Montgomery, Jas., labr.
344 to 354 Vacant ground

193 Huey, R., fruiterer
195 Gallagher, Mrs. Rose A., agent Monarch laundry
197 Kennan, Margt., conf.
....*Ballycastle st intersects*.....
199 Gibson, W., grocer
201 M'Mordie, Mrs. Martha
203 Hurley, Kath., dressmkr
205 Walker, Wm., labourer
207 Duff, Mrs. Jane
209 Wilson, J., breadserver
.....*Ballynure st intersects*....
211 Jones, Robt., grocer
213 Synott, Peter, tailor
215 Lyons, A., motor mchnc
217 Gallagher, Mrs. Brigid
219 Devlin, Mrs. Sarah, agt
.....*Ballyclare st intersects*......
221-223 Ferguson Bros., grocers
225 Haughey, Wm., plasterer
227 M'Keown, Miss Agnes
229 Adams, John, electrician
231 Stewart, Mrs. Mary
233 Welch, R., labourer
235 Orr, James J., breadsvr.
237 Gault, Robt., joiner
239 Culbert, C., motordvr.
241 M'Claverty, Miss D.
243 Hay, Wm., fitter
245 Steen, Mary, confectionr
.... *Oldpark av intersects*.
247, 249 Kennedy, J., grocer
251 Blair, W.
253 May, Edmund, rivetter
255 Mahood, Mrs. Mary E.
257 Cuningham, G., sheet metal worker
259 M'Cleave, Thos. J., fitter
261 M'Crudden, Thos. Irwin, boilermaker

263 Campbell, A., labourer
265 Richardson, A., coachbuilder
267 Minnis, Andw., blrmkr.
269 Adrain, John, plater
285, 287 Finiston P.E.S.— J. C. Connell, principal
289 Payne, Mrs. Mina
291 Owens, Mrs. M.
293 Tilley, E.
...*Heathfield rd intersects*...
295 Carson, D., rivetter
297 Wilson, Jas., finisher
299 Shannon, Mrs. Margt.
301 M'Cormick, Jos., mangr.
301a M'Cormick, Hugh G., rigger
...*Torrens ave intersects*...
Vacant ground
319 Martin, Jas. P., foreman
321 Clarke, James, labr.
323 Baird, Robert
325 Cockcroft, R.
327 M'Guiggan, Wm., joiner
329 Little, L., linen business
331 Kennedy, Jos., overlooker
333 Wilson, John, plumber
335 Sudway, Leo., mechanic
337 Johnston, Geo., carrier
339 Fagan, Finton, travlr.
341 Bamford, William
343 Williamson, J. H., electn
345 Peyton, Alex., comp.
347 Logier, Mrs. R., music teacher
349 Marshall, Mrs. Mary
Vacant ground
Oldpark Farmyard intersects
371 Byron Recreation Club
373 Snoddy, E., confctrn.

375 M'Cafferty, Miss Ruth
377 Ramsey, Robt., labourer
379 Paul, Aaron
381 Bradley, John, labr.
383 Kennedy, Robt., labr.
385 Forde, W. J., shoemkr.
387 Bratty, Waddell J., moulder
389 Cameron, Charles
391 Semple, Mrs. Elizabeth
393 Bonnar, Mrs. Elizabeth
395 English, Mrs. Mary
397 Lee, Chas. Ed., labr.
399 M'Kinley, Geo., window cleaner
401 Clegg, John, labourer
403 Houston, T., painter
405 Telford, Robt., window cleaner
407 Redpath, Andw., labr.
409 Hartley, John, electrcn.
411 Paul, Joseph, labourer
413 Campbell, Wm., labourer
415 Blakely, Mrs. M. E.
417 Coleman, George, clerk
419 M'Callum, G.
421 Paul, John, labourer
423 Paul, J., labourer
425 Esler, Mrs. Annie
427 Crawford, Mrs. M.
Vacant Ground
...*Torrens ave intersects*...
...*Torrens pde intersects*...

Oldpark Farm Yard
OFF OLDPARK ROAD.
Clifton, N. Belfast (U.K.): Clifton (N.I.).
1 Hewitt, Annie
2 Shaw, Mrs. Anna
3 Kernoghan, Sarah
4 Watson, Saml., labourer
5 Jackson, Mrs. Bessie
6 Watson, Saml., driver
7 Glover, James, labr.

Lower Lodge Av.
OFF OLDPARK ROAD.
Clifton, N. Belfast (U.K.). Oldpark (N.I.).
Lower Lodge Factory—J. S. Brown & Sons, Ltd.

Ardilea Street

OFF OLDPARK ROAD.

Clifton, N. Belfast (U.K.);
Oldpark (N.I.).

1 M'Kee, —
3 Cassidy, Susan
5 M'Laughlin, P., musician
7 Carlin, Mrs.
9 Saunders, Jos., labourer
11 Mulholland, Patk., labr.
13 Law, Maggie, stitcher
15 Delargy, Maggie
17 Clark, James
19 M'Ateer, W., labourer
21 M'Nally, John, labourer
23 Gordon, S., labourer
27 to 33 CITY BAKERY CO.
  (BELFAST), LIMITED.
  'Phone 2015.
35 Vacant
37 Kavanagh, B., labourer
39 Mahoney, Mrs. B.
41 Mahoney, Mrs.
43 O'Reilly, Francis
45 Mulholland, Chas., labr.
47 Caulfield, Bernard, labr.
49 M'Alinden, W., labourer
Vacant ground
61 Hyndman, Wm., seaman
63 Daly, Mrs. Mary
65 M'Guigan, Peter, hackler
67 Collins, John, labourer
69 Toman, Mrs. Mary
71 Wallace, A., labourer
73 Maguire, Miss Mary
75 Grimley, Mrs.

77 Caulfield, Miss Mary
79 Coucher, Thos., labourer
81 Mulholland, W. J., labr.
83 Thomas, Mary
85 Boyle, Annie
87 Quinn, Mrs. Mary
89 Toner, Joseph, labourer
91 Dick, Isaiah, labourer
93 Cochrane, Thos., labourer
95 Killen, W. J., labr.
97 Bateson, Wm. James
99 M'Cannister, James
101 Brooks, William
103 Daly, W.J., flax dresser
105 Grego, Jeremiah, labr.
107 Rafter, Richard
109 M'Quade, Miss Ellen
111 Cathcart, Margaret
113 Connolly, Eliza
115 M'Cool, Wm., shop assnt
117 Kearney, John, labourer

—

2 Rooney, Lilian
4 Crossey, J., heater
6 M'Guire, J., labourer
8 M'Connell, Edwd., labr.
10 Clarke, S., smithshelper
12 Hughes, John, labourer
14 Gorman, James, fitter
16 M'Intyre, George, labr.
18 Kane, Henry, rougher
20 M'Allister, John, joiner
22 M'Callister, Mrs. Jane
24 Seawright, Thos., rougher
26 O'Connor, James, flaxdsr
28 Sullivan, Thomas
30 Thomas, Wm., labourer

32 Clarke, John, labourer
34 Dunlop, Mrs. M.
36 Gallagher, John, seaman
38 Douglas, James
40 Mackin, Jas., bootmaker
42 Campbell, Mrs. Rose
44 Moynes, John, labourer
46 Stewart, Chas., labourer
48 O'Donnell, —
50 Lappin, Patrick, labr.
52 M'Auley, Thos., labourer
54 Service, John, moulder
56 Dargan, Mrs. Maggie
58 Kerr, Alex., steel erector
60 M'Veigh, Annie
62 Mathers, Matthew, rghr.
64 Terrin, Joseph, labourer
66 Collins, Denis, musician
......Glenpark st intersects.....
68-70 Merniel, John A., grcr.
72 Matthews, Patk., labr.
72a Brougham, Patrick
74 M'Geough, Margaret
74a M'Geough, B.
76 Freel, Joseph
76a Daly, Ellen
78 Quinn, Mrs. Annie
78a Donnelly, Mrs. Maggie
80 M'Cracken, John, flaxdrsr
82 M'Keown, John, labr.
82a M'Cann, Edward
84 Murphy, John, labourer
84a M'Grath, Patrick
86 Smith, Kathleen
86a Quinn, Patrick
88 Cooke, Susan
88a Smith, Susan

90 Henry, Mrs.
90a Bloomfield, John, labr.
92 O'Connor, Edwd., striker
94 Savage, John, labourer
94a Mahoney, Samuel
96 M'Caffrey, Bernard
98 Bloomfield, Margt., spnnr
100 Cunningham, C., spinner
102 Halfpenny, J., labourer
102a Cord, Mrs. Brigid
104 O'Neill, Mrs. Maria
106 Gallagher, H., tailor
108 Quinn, John, labourer
110 Griffith, John, joiner
112 M'Guigan, Bernard, labr
114 Campbell, Dan
116 Garland, B., rougher
118 Clarke, Henry, labourer
120 Kerr, Patk., flaxdresser
122 Donnelly, Patrick, labr.
124 Deans, Mrs.
126 M'Glade, Mrs.
128 M'Killen, Miss Rose
130 Killen, Mrs. Catherine
132 M'Taggart, P., labourer
134 M'Killen, Jas., flaxdrsr.
136 Kinney, Mrs. Elizabeth
138 Campbell, S., sweeper
140 M'Crudden, Jas., labr.
142 O'Neill, Margt., spinner
144 Smyth, Wm., labourer
146 Smith, Patrick, rougher
148 Morrow, Mrs. Sarah

Gracehill Street

FROM OLDPARK ROAD TO
GLENVIEW STREET.

Clifton, N. Belfast (U.K.);
Oldpark (N.I.).

1 Side door
3 Evans, Mrs. Catherine
5 Crudden, Mrs.
7 Crudden, Patk., carter
9 Forsythe, Mrs. Matilda
Sacred Heart Parochial Hall
15 O'Brien Jos., clerk
17 Osborne, Jas., porter
19 Connolly, Thos., Customs
21 Mathers, Mrs. Mary
23 O'Kane, Patk., dealer
25 M'Ewan, Mrs. Mary
27 Cassidy, P., labourer
29 Healey, Thomas, labourer
31 Trainor, Elizabeth
33 M'Mahon, Wm., joiner
35 M'Keown, Patk., labourer
37 Hughes, Jas., labourer
39 M'Poland, Jane
41 Convery, J., bleacher
47 Gateway
49 Hunter, Hugh, carter
51 M'Groarty, Wm., labr.
53 Gateway
55 M'Gorrity, M., labourer
57 Rainey, Thos., labr.
59, 61 Gateway
63 Cravaghan, Henry, labr.
65 Rogan, F., fish tackle mkr
67, 69 Gateway

71 Roberts, Wm., labourer
73 M'Phillips, Danl., labr.
75 M'Aleenenan, Jas., dealer
77 Stewart, Frank, labourer
79 Hurst, Amelia
81 Donnelly, Mrs. Mary J.
83 Mulholland, R., labourer
85 M'Cafferty, Saml., lab'rer
87 M'Donald, Bridget
89 Murray, Alice
91 Rocks, Mrs. Bridgid
93 Barnes, Margaret
95 M'Cann, Wm., labourer
97 Boyles, Robt., labourer
99 Ferron, Wm., labourer

2 M'Gahen, P., labourer
4 Irvine, G., labourer
6 Seawright, Miss Lizzie
8 Devenny, Alex, joiner
10 Corrigan, Mary
12 Sheridan, Edward, store
  man
14 Burns, J., seaman
16 Mulvenna, P., warder
18 O'Hara, Robt. James
20 Rooney, John
22 Shields, Peter, carter
24 Crockford, Jas., labourer
26 Coyle, Miss Annie
28 Vacant
30 Fitzpatrick, J., fireman
32 Pimley, Wm., baker
34 Spence, David, clerk
36 Heatley, Jas., labourer
38 Ritchie, Robert

40 Hughes, Frank, flaxdressr.
42 Lucas, Mrs. Margaret
44 Mulholland, Jas., labr.
44a Fenton, Bert
46 Toal, Michael, clerk
48 M'Laughlin, Gerald, milk
  vendor
50 Grego, Geo., coal vendor

Mayfair Street

FROM OLDPARK ROAD TO
GRACEHILL STREET.

Clifton, N. Belfast (U.K.);
Oldpark (N.I.).

1 Donnelly, Frank, labourer
3 Magee, J., hackler
5 Sheridan, Thos., manager
7 Smith, James, labourer
9 M'Aleary, J., irondresser
11 Wade, S., labourer
13 Shannon, Christopher
15 Mulvenna, Chas., labourer
17 Magill, Mrs. Catherine
19 Moore, Walter, labr.
21 Powers, L., watchman
23 Creen, Wm., shoemaker
25 Arbuckle, Wm., labourer
27 Morrison, Miss Hannah
29 Somerville, Jas., waiter
31 M'Intyre, G., labourer
33 M'Laughlin, Mrs. Margt.
35 Sheppard, Robert
37 Boggett, J. E.
39 M'Dowell, J., labourer
41 M'Lean, James
43 Clarke, J., machinist

45 Topping, Geo., labourer
47 Topping, Saml., labr.
49 Steele, J., caretaker
51 Todd, F., bellows maker
53 Young, Mrs. M., fruiterer

—

2 Henry, Mrs. Jane
4 M'Auley, Terence, hair-
  dresser
6 M'Mahon, John
8 Grimley, John, labourer
10 Rafferty, Jas. Francis
12 Magill, R. T., carter
14 Reilly, Mrs. Ellen
16 Donnelly, James, labourer
18 Gearnon, Mrs. Kate
20 M'Laverty, Henry, labr.
22 Murray, John, flaxdsr.
24 Boucher, Miss Mary
26 M'Allister, John, joiner
28 Loughran, Jas., labourer
30 Sterling, William
32 Leslie, Thomas
34 Corrigan, Michael, electrician
36 O'Neill, Geo., labourer
38 M'Kenna, Joseph, barman
40 Smith, John
42 Toal, Michael, labourer
44 M'Veigh, Jas., labourer
46 Murray, F., labourer
48 Morrison, John, labourer
50 Fields, Mrs. Mary Ann
52 Hughes, Bella
54 Collins, Patk., labourer
56 O'Kane, John, labourer

Havana Street

OFF ARDOYNE AV.

Clifton, N. Belfast (U.K.);
Oldpark (N.I.).

....Kingston st intersects....

1 Jeffers, James, shop asst.
3 Quinn, Michael, poultry dealer
5 Sherlock, A., dressmkr.
7 Mollan, Mrs. Mary
9 Hood, Mrs. Ellen
11 Dogherty, J., labourer
13 M'Kenna, Mrs.
15 Conlon, Miss
17 Gilvary, W. J., civ. srvt.
19 M'Donnell, Margaret
21 French, J., porter
23 Heaney, John, labourer
25 Lafferty, R., flax dresser
27 French, Martin, porter
29 Laverty, John, butcher
31 Cousins, Sarah Margaret
33 M'Crystal, Francis, driver
35 Cash, Mary
37 M'Callum, Thomas
39 Monaghan, J. P., civil svt.
41 Barr, Saml., joiner
43 Prenter, Wm., polisher
45 Scallan, Joseph, clerk

......Manilla st intersects......

47, 49 Donaldson, F. P., groc
51 M'Loughlin, T., joiner
53 M'Cullough, Josephine
55 Holland, Thos., labourer
57 White, Ed., labourer

59 Grieve, Thomas
61 Wilson, R., telephone wkr
63 Montgomery, J., fitter
65 O'Brien, Sarah
67 Crumley, C. T.
69 Tiernan, Mary Ellen

......Jamaica st intersects......

2 Toal, Sarah, confectioner
4 Mallaghan, B., dealer
6 M'Kenna, J., barman
8 M'Grogan, Mary
10 Toal, Jas., labourer
12 Morgan, Chas., joiner
14 Goan, Mrs.
16 Drake, F., painter
18 M'Cann, Miss
20 Wilson, J., clerk
22 Cullen, Wm., labourer
24 Taylor, Joseph, butcher
26 M'Cusker, H., manager
28 Kerr, Daniel
30 Flannery, D. J., postman
32 M'Conville, Alice
34 M'Cartan, Annie
36 Clarke, Francis, barman
38 Taylor, P.
40 Heaney, Mrs.
42 Gorman, Thos., barman
44 M'Laverty, F., lab
46 Sparkes, J. P., butcher
48 Grealey, M., labourer
50 Cannon, John, clerk
52 Maguire, John
54 Quinn, Alice
56 Keenan, Thos, labourer

58 Davie, Bridget
60 Higgins, Edward, travlr.
62 Bryant, Geo., motorman
64 Gallagher, M., barman
66 M'Cartan, Patk., joiner
68 Denny, C., coachpainter
70 Hopkins, Ellen
72 M'Ilmunn, Charles, labr.
74 M'Kee, Susan
76 Heazley, Thos., labourer
78 Dickson, J., labourer
80 M'Kee, R., labourer
82 Mulvenny, John
84 Smith, Robt., labourer
86 M'Gurk, Bernard, labr.
88 Neeson, Thos., tailor
90 M'Kane, A., motorman
92 Marley, Margaret
94 Sheridan, Edw., labourer

Kingston Street

AT 1 HAVANA STREET.

Clifton, N. Belfast (U.K.);
Oldpark (N.I.).

2 O'Hare, Thos., labourer
4 Cairns, Mrs. Elizabeth
6 Heaney, J. R., labourer
8 Timothy, Thos., labourer
10 Wilson, David, labourer
12 Lavery, Jack
14 Doherty, Thos., labourer
16 Johnston, J., labourer
18 M'Callan, Mrs. Catherine
20 Myles, Patk., labourer
22 Magee, Jane
24 Hughes, John, labourer
26 Donnelly, Wm., labourer

Glenpark Street

FROM LOUISA STREET TO
ARDILEA STREET.

Clifton, N. Belfast (U.K.);
Oldpark (N.I.).

1a O'Kane, John, carpenter
5 M'Hugh, Miss E., grocer
7 Sherdin, Thos., labourer
7 M'Gann, Thos., dealer
9 Watson, Jos., painter

......Glenview st intersects......

.....Antigua st intersects.....

2, 4 Connolly, P., publicn.
6 M'Guiness, Wm., labourer
8 Ardis, John
10 Brown, John, labourer
12 O'Neill, W. J., labourer
14 Marley, Mrs. Ann Jane
16 M'Kernan, Peter
18 Patterson, David, labr.
20 Martin, Hugh, labourer
22 Mollan, Elizabeth, spinr.
34 Matthewson, Mrs. Cath.
36 Caufield, Jas., labourer
38 M'Anally, Robt., labr.
40, 42 O'Carroll Bros., grcrs

Antigua Street

FROM GLENPARK ST. TO
EWART'S ROW.

Clifton, N. Belfast (U.K.);
Oldpark (N.I.).

...Saunderson st intersects...

Crawford, —, stable

Glenview Street

FROM OLDPARK ROAD TO
GLENPARK STREET.

Clifton, N. Belfast (U.K.);
Oldpark (N.I.).

1a Sacred Heart R.C. Chapel
  —Rev. J. M'Auley, P.P.;
  Rev. J. Connor, C.C.;
  Rev. L. M'Keown, B.A.,
  C.C.
1 Collins, Mrs. Mary
3 M'Guiness, A., labourer
5 Dickie, John, ins. collector
7 Beattie, Saml., labourer
9 M'Allenan, Jas., labr.
11 Murray, John, labourer
13 O'Connor, John, labourer
15 Davison, Joseph, carrier
17 Hunter, Mrs. Mary
19 Fagan, Jas., labourer
21 Fagan, Hugh, labourer
23 Owens, John, labourer
25 Sullivan, T., labourer
27 Mooney, Margaret
29 M'Cullough, Patk., labr
31 M'Phillips, Wm., printer
33 Gillan, Thos., joiner
35 Crawford, John, dealer
37 Kearney, Jas., labourer
39 Crossey, W., labourer

2 Delaney, Charles, news-vendor

4 M'Dade, Mrs. Bella
6 Shields, Thos., labourer
8 Farren, John
10 Barr, Patrick
12 Mulholland, John, labr.
14 Cassidy, John, labourer
16 Hamill, Mrs.
18 Gillan, Bridget
20 Dickey, Jos., labourer
22 Tierney, Mary
24 M'Intaggart, Mrs.
26 Toner, Bridget
28 Gall, Lean, labourer
30 Crawford, Michael
32 Donnelly, John
34 Muldoon, Patk., labourer
36 Moans, Mrs.
38 Dogherty, Edwd., labr.
40 Speight, C., paper maker
40a Bean. & Co., boiler and
  steam-pipe coverers
42 Savage, Mrs. Catherine
St. Columban's Public Elem.
  Schools — J. Beckett,
  principal of boys; Miss
  A. Doran, prin. of girls
52 Fitzsimmons, Mrs. C.,
  grocer
54 M'Loughlin, Wm., dealer
56 Mulgrave, John, labourer
58 Goodfellow, Patk., dealer

Parkview Street

FROM OLDPARK ROAD TO
GRACEHILL STREET.

Clifton, N. Belfast (U.K.);
Oldpark (N.I.).

1 O'Hara, Chas., flaxdresser
3 M'Keown, Jas., labourer
5 Donaghy, Jas., labourer
7 Shields, Mrs. Mary
9 Ferran, Edward
11 Murphy, Mrs. Catherine
13 Hughes, Henry, labourer
15 Toman, Mrs.
17 Murphy, Patrick
19 Wallwin, Jas., shop ass't
21 Murphy, John, carter
23 Humphrey, Mrs.
25 M'Gowan, Mrs. Annie
27 Morrison, Wm., labourer
29 O'Rawe, Chas., fireman
31 Byrne, Wm., flaxdresser
33 M'Guire, Thos., dealer
35 Carmichael, Wm., labr.
37 Burns, Mrs. Mary
39 Morrison, Patk., labr.
41 Kane, James, rougher
43 Rutledge, Mrs. Maggie
45 M'Kearnan, Patk., labr
47 Scullion, Mrs. Ellen
49 Owens, Mrs. Kate
51 Smyth, James, carter
53 M'Cann, Hugh, rivetter
55 M'Nally, Saml., labourer

2 Smyth, Catherine
4 Rogan, Mrs.
6 Smith, Henry, labourer
8 Burns, Bernard, labourer
10 M'Ginn, H., labourer
12 Burns, Daniel, labourer
14 Loughran, Mrs.
16 Delaney, Patrick
18 Stewart, Charles, porter
20 Morrison, Geo., labourer
22 M'Clean, Jas., labourer
24 Murphy, Francis, labr.
26 Loughran, Mrs.
28 Barnes, Wm., labourer
30 Mahoney, Patk., labr.
32 Crilly, Mrs. Catherine
34 Cavana, Mrs. Matilda
36 M'Garry, Mrs.
38 M'Gibben, J., labourer
40 Morrison, Chas., labr.

Saunderson Street

OFF ANTIGUA STREET.

Clifton, N. Belfast (U.K.);
Oldpark (N.I.).

2 Woods, John, tailor
4 Corr, Jos., labr.
6 Allister, Mrs. M.
8 Reilly, Ellen
10 Simpson, Patk., labourer
12 M'Cabe, Charles

CHARLES BELL (1963) LTD.
344 OLDPARK ROAD, BELFAST
(TRADE ONLY)

Super Verticals   Super Venetians   Super Rollers

A DISTRICT CALLED

THE BONE

**is the first publication in a series of historical studies
on working class districts of Belfast**

In Preparation

**ARDOYNE
NEW LODGE
SHORT STRAND
CARRICK HILL
THE SHANKILL**

JAMES MURRAY
BOOKMAKER
Est. 1928

OLDPARK ROAD	**BANK LANE**
BELFAST	**BANGOR**
TELEPHONE 351335	**TELEPHONE 91 472717**

Wishing
Glenravel Local History Project
Every Success
With Their New Publication

A DISTRICT CALLED
THE BONE

Flax Fuels

Flax Centre   Ardoyne Avenue
Tel. 741891   -   DELIVERIES.

BURNGLO   £2.89

EMBERGLO   £2.80

EXTRACITE   £4.45

TOWER ESSE   £3.59

ESSE NUTS   £4.00

5 STAR COAL   £2.50

DOUBLES   £2.25

WONDER COAL   £3.10

COLITE   £3.99

COCLITE   £3.65

P/CITE   £4.45

SLACK   £2.00

RED FLAME   £3.25

BEANS   £3.69

GRAINS   £3.29

OPEN
MON -SAT
9 a.m.6p.m

OPEN LATE
THURS & FRI
9a.m. - 9p.m.

PATRICIA'S

251 OLDPARK ROAD

GROCERIES, CARDS, CONFECTIONARY & COAL

SELECTION
OF
DAILY NEWSPAPERS

WARM AND FRIENDLY
SERVICE
WITH A SMILE

COME IN AND LOOK AROUND

COOPER CHEMISTS

**157 OLDPARK ROAD
BELFAST BT14 6QP
PHONE: 351506**

*Your Community
Pharmacy For
Our 30 Years*

Complete
Pharmaceutical Service
Available

ROONEY BUTCHERS

161 OLDPARK ROAD

*WELL
ESTABLISHED
FAMILY BUTCHER
IN THE
BONE*

'FAMOUS FOR
OUR SAUSAGES'

PARK TAXIS

247 OLDPARK ROAD

FAST AND EFFICIENT
SERVICE

PHONE:
746746

ALL OUR CARS ARE
RADIO CONTROLLED

THE MULVENNA ACADEMY OF IRISH DANCING

TUITION BY: *BRENDA MULVENNA*
&
DEBORAH MULVENNA-MURPHY

CLASSES HELD EVERY SATURDAY

10.30 A.M. - 12.30 P.M.
IN THE
SACRED HEART PARISH CENTRE

NEW PUPILS WELCOME

Wine Flair

FOR A WIDE SELECTION OF SPIRITS, WINES, AND BEERS

AT COMPETITIVE PRICES

Hairdressing Salon

Rumours
165A Oldpark Road

SPECIAL O.A.P. EVERY TUES
PERM £8.00 SHAMPOO /SET £2.00
CUT /SHAMPOO /SET £3.00
DULCIA PERM from £12.00

(FREE CONDITIONER TREATMENT
WORTH £2.00 WITH EVERY PERM)

EYE-BROW WAXING £2.25
RESTYLE WASH AND
BLOW DRY £5.50
KID'S TRIMS £2.00
OPEN TUES. - SAT.
NO CUSTOM EVER REFUSED

Proprietor Briege.

BEECHFIELD MOTOR WORKS

PARK PICTURE HOUSE BUILDING
OLDPARK ROAD
TEL. 740361

CAR AND VAN SALES
CAR AND COMMERCIAL,
SALES AND REPAIRS
M.O.T. and P.S.V. SPECIALISTS

SHAUNA'S

209 OLDPARK ROAD

**YOUR LOCAL CORNER SHOP
CATERING FOR ALL
YOUR GROCERY NEEDS**

FRESH BREAD
AND
DAILY BARGAINS

OPEN 8.00 a.m TO LATE
7 DAYS PER WEEK

THE NITE BITE

249 Oldpark Road

FRESH FISH AND CHIPS DAILY
HOME-MADE PASTIES
CHICKEN BREASTS AND LEGS
DONER KEBABS, SAUSAGES,
BEEFBURGERS, CHICKEN
FILLET BURGERS

DONER CHIP AND GRAVY
SPECIAL
VARIOUS OTHER HOT
FOODS AND A VARIETY OF
SPECIALS

**OPEN EACH DAY
1200 p.m. to 2.00 a.m.
DELIVERIES
12.00 - 2.00 p.m. MON- FRI
4.00 p.m.- 2.00 a.m. SAT&SUN**

FLAX LAUNDRY
DRY CLEANERS+SHOE REPAIRS

Open 6 Days a Week 9a.m.- 5p.m

THE FLAX LAUNDRY CAN
NOW OFFER OUR CUSTOMERS
A FULL HOUSEHOLD SERVICE
WITHOUT LEAVING THE
COMFORT
OF YOUR OWN HOME

FOR A PROMPT AND RELIABLE
SERVICE AT KEEN RATES
RING OR JUST CALL IN

FLAX CENTRE, BELFAST
TEL: 351571

All sorts of Commercial Laundry including
hairdressers, factory, hotels etc. accepted.

THINK-A-HEAD

UNISEX HAIR SALON

FLAX CENTRE TEL. 745440

Ladies

TUES - FRI. 9 a.m. - 5 p.m.
SATURDAY 9 a.m. - 5 p.m.

Gents (Seamy Teer)

TUES - FRI. 10 a.m. - 5 p.m.
SATURDAY 10 a.m. - 5 p.m.

PRICES HARD TO BEAT

Flowers for All Occasions

Marian's Flower Corner

UNIT 10 FLAX CENTRE
TEL. 0232 740196

Fresh Flowers and Plants
Baby Arrangements
Funeral Sprays
Wedding Flowers

Religious Articles
Cards and Irish Souvenirs

WE DELIVER TO ALL AREAS
INTERNATIONAL
DELIVERIES
NOW AVAILABLE
'TELEFLORIST'

MURPHY'S
ARDOYNE AVENUE

FOR ALL YOUR
GROCERY NEEDS

NEWSAGENTS
AND
CONFECTIONERS

OPEN
8 a.m. to late
EVERY DAY